ii

THE GRACIOUS SOCIETY

HUMANIZING AI FOR A BETTER WORLD

SERGIO MARES

For Virgie,
My inspiration, My Hope, My Forever Love

CONTENTS

Preface: A Gracious Society   *ix*
Introduction: Empathy, Compassion, Unity   *xii*
    The Potential of AI   *xv*

PART 1: THE FOUNDATIONS OF A GRACIOUS SOCIETY

Human Dignity	2
Human Dignity in Practice	5
Solidarity	9
Examples of Solidarity	12
Subsidiarity and Empowerment	15
Examples of Subsidiarity and Empowerment	18
The Common Good	21
Policies and Practices	24
The Preferential Option for the Poor	28

PART II: AI TECHNOLOGY AND ITS ROLE IN A GRACIOUS SOCIETY

AI for Social Good	34
AI in Healthcare	37

AI Healthcare Ethical Considerations	40
AI Education	42
AI Education: Equal Access	45
AI and Environmental Sustainability	49
AI Climate Change	52
Ethical AI Development	55
AI and Job Opportunities	59
AI Driven Workforce	63

PART III: BUILDING A GRACIOUS SOCIETY IN THE ERA OF AI

Fostering a Culture of Encounter	67
Strategies for Promoting a Culture of Encounter	70
Collaborative Efforts	75
Individual Actions	80
Ways to Contribute	84
Afterward	*87*
Recommended Reading	*91*
Reference	*93*

Preface
A GRACIOUS SOCIETY

I would like to share a vision. A vision of hope, unity, and compassion—a Gracious Society. In a world fraught with division, strife, and seemingly insurmountable challenges, the idea of a Gracious Society might seem like an unattainable dream. But I am here to tell you that it is not only possible, it is essential. And with the remarkable advances in artificial intelligence, we have the opportunity to transform this vision into a reality.

A Gracious Society is one that upholds the dignity of every human being, regardless of race, gender, religion, or socioeconomic status. It is a society that believes in the power of human connection and collaboration, where we stand in solidarity with one another in our shared pursuit of a better world. It is a society that embraces the principles of subsidiarity and empowerment, where the voices of individuals and communities are heard, respected, and given the opportunity to shape their own destinies.

In this Gracious Society, we prioritize the common good, striving to create a world where everyone has the chance to thrive and contribute to the greater whole. We are guided by a profound commitment to the poor and vulnerable, recognizing that their well-being is intrinsically linked to our own, and that lifting them up is not an act of charity, but an act of justice. To achieve this Gracious Society, we must come together and harness the power of one of the most revolutionary forces of our time: artificial intelligence. As the capabilities of AI continue to expand at an unprecedented pace, we have a unique opportunity to use this technology to build bridges, foster empathy, and strengthen the bonds that connect us.

Imagine a world where AI is used to predict and prevent diseases, personalizing treatments to ensure that every individual has the best chance at a healthy life. Picture a world where AI-powered education systems adapt to each student's unique needs, ensuring that every child has the opportunity to reach their full potential. Envision a world where AI helps us monitor and protect our environment, conserving resources and safeguarding the planet for future generations.

But the transformative potential of AI is not without its challenges. As we embrace this technology, we must also confront the ethical dilemmas it presents, ensuring that the development and deployment of AI align with our values and uphold the principles of a Gracious Society. We must strive for fairness, transparency, and accountability in AI, ensuring that these systems do not perpetuate existing inequalities, but instead work to dismantle them.

To create a Gracious Society in the age of AI, we must foster a culture of encounter—a culture where we actively seek out the perspectives of those who are different from us, where we listen with open hearts and minds, and where we engage in meaningful dialogue that bridges the divides that separate us. Pope Francis has called us to embrace this culture of encounter, reminding us that it is through our connections with one another that we find the strength and inspiration to build a better world.

As we embark on this journey, we must remember that the Gracious Society is not the responsibility of any single individual, organization, or government. It is the collective responsibility of all of us, each and every one of us, to work together in pursuit of this vision. It is through our shared commitment to empathy, compassion, and understanding that we can overcome the challenges that lie ahead and create a world where everyone has the opportunity to flourish.

So, I ask you today: Will you join me in this quest for a Gracious Society? Will you stand with me in the pursuit of a more compassionate, inclusive world, powered by the incredible potential of artificial intelligence? Together, we can make the dream of a Gracious Society a reality, and in doing so, we can leave a lasting, positive impact on the lives of countless individuals across the globe.

In the coming years, the decisions we make and the actions we take will define the trajectory of our society. Let us choose the path of empathy, compassion, and unity. Let us embrace the power of artificial intelligence to address our most pressing challenges and build a world where every person has the opportunity to thrive. Let our shared vision of a Gracious Society inspire us to act with courage, determination, and an unwavering belief in the power of human connection. Together, we can create a brighter, more connected future for all.

Thank you for joining me on this journey, and I hope that each of you will take this message to heart and become an agent of change in your own communities. Let us work together to make the Gracious Society a reality, using the incredible power of AI to uplift humanity and bring us closer together than ever before. In this spirit, I invite you to continue the conversation, engage with others, and explore the incredible potential of AI and its role in fostering a Gracious Society. Let's work together to shape a world that reflects our highest aspirations and ensures that no one is left behind.

INTRODUCTION:
Empathy, Compassion, Unity

We're at a critical moment in our shared history. A moment that calls for reflection, action, and a renewed commitment to the values that have the power to bring us together and shape a brighter future: empathy, compassion, and unity. In a world that is increasingly polarized, where division and discord too often take center stage, it is essential that we recognize and embrace the transformative power of empathy, compassion, and unity. I invite you on a journey o11f discovery and inspiration, as we explore the importance of these values in our lives and the world at large.

Empathy, the ability to understand and share the feelings of another, is a cornerstone of our humanity. It is the bridge that connects us, enabling us to see the world through the eyes of others, and to recognize the commonalities that bind us together. In today's world, where we are bombarded with information and opinions, it can be all too easy to retreat into our own echo chambers and lose sight of the perspectives of those who are different from us. But empathy is a powerful antidote to this isolation, reminding us of the beauty and richness that comes from truly engaging with the experiences and viewpoints of others. Empathy is the starting point for compassion, the deep and genuine concern for the suffering and well-being of others.

Compassion is a force that transcends borders and cultures, inspiring us to act in the service of those in need. It is the wellspring of kindness, generosity, and love that has the power to heal our world and bridge the divides that separate us. In a time when we are confronted with unprecedented challenges

– from poverty and inequality to climate change and conflict – it is our collective capacity for compassion that will determine our ability to rise to the occasion and create a better future for all.

Unity, the state of being one, is the culmination of empathy and compassion, and the foundation upon which we can build a more just and equitable world. Unity does not require us to abandon our differences or homogenize our cultures. Rather, it asks us to recognize the inherent interconnectedness of our lives and destinies, and to work together in pursuit of a common good that transcends our individual interests. Unity is not simply an ideal, but a pragmatic and necessary approach to addressing the complex, global challenges that we face today.

Now, you might ask, how do we cultivate empathy, compassion, and unity in a world that often seems determined to drive us apart? How do we foster these values in the face of fear, uncertainty, and division? I believe that the answer lies in the choices we make every day – the way we engage with one another, the conversations we have, the stories we tell, and the actions we take.

To cultivate empathy, we must be willing to step outside our comfort zones and truly listen to the perspectives of others. We must engage in open and honest dialogue, embracing the vulnerability that comes from acknowledging our own biases and blind spots. We must seek out stories that challenge and inspire us, stories that remind us of our shared humanity and the common threads that bind us together.

To foster compassion, we must recognize the suffering of others and be moved to act in their service. We must make a conscious effort to extend kindness and understanding, even when it is difficult or uncomfortable. We must also be compassionate with ourselves, recognizing that our own well-being is intrinsically linked to the well-being of others, and that self-care is an essential foundation for a compassionate life.

And to build unity, we must be willing to stand together in the face of adversity, finding strength in our shared values and aspirations. We must forge partnerships and alliances across borders, cultures, and political divides, recognizing that our collective wisdom and power is far greater than the sum of our individual efforts. We must also be champions for inclusivity, ensuring that every voice is heard, and that the solutions we pursue are truly representative of the diverse needs and aspirations of our global community.

In embracing empathy, compassion, and unity, we have the power to create a world that is kinder, more just, and more resilient. A world where the challenges we face are not met with fear and division, but with hope, collaboration, and an unwavering belief in the power of our shared humanity. So, I ask each of you reading this book to join me in this mission to cultivate empathy, compassion, and unity in our lives and in our world. Let us be the change we wish to see, and in doing so, let us inspire others to join us on this journey. Let this be the beginning of a global movement, a movement grounded in empathy, fueled by compassion, and driven by a shared commitment to unity. For it is in these values that we find the strength and inspiration to build a better world, a world where every individual has the opportunity to thrive, and where our collective well-being takes precedence over our individual pursuits. Together, we have the power to shape a brighter future for ourselves and for generations to come. Let us seize this opportunity, and let us never forget that the power to create a better world lies within each and every one of us.

The Potential of AI

We stand at the precipice of a new era—an era defined by remarkable technological advancements that have the potential to reshape our world in ways previously unimaginable. At the heart of this revolution lies artificial intelligence, or AI, a powerful and transformative force that is already changing the way we live, work, and interact with one another. As we embark on this exciting journey, we must ask ourselves: How can we harness the incredible potential of AI to foster a Gracious Society, a society defined by empathy, compassion, and unity? I invite you to join me as we explore this question and imagine a future where AI is not only a tool for progress, but a catalyst for a more just, equitable, and compassionate world.

AI is a technology that is advancing at an unprecedented pace, rapidly surpassing our wildest dreams and opening up new realms of possibility. From healthcare to education, transportation to environmental conservation, AI is revolutionizing the way we approach some of our most pressing challenges, and in doing so, is paving the way for a Gracious Society.

Imagine a world where AI-powered healthcare systems can predict and prevent diseases, personalizing treatments to ensure that every individual has the best chance at a healthy life. Picture a world where AI-driven education adapts to each student's unique needs and learning styles, ensuring that every child has the opportunity to reach their full potential. Envision a world where AI helps us monitor and protect our environment, conserving resources and safeguarding the planet for future generations.

But the potential of AI in fostering a Gracious Society extends far beyond these practical applications. AI has the power to bring people together, bridging divides and fostering empathy and understanding among diverse communities. By developing AI systems that can understand and process natural language, we can break down barriers to communication, enabling people from different cultures and backgrounds to connect with one another in ways never before possible. AI can also play a critical role in addressing the challenges of bias and discrimination that continue to plague our societies. By designing AI systems that are fair, transparent, and accountable, we can work to dismantle systemic inequalities and ensure that the benefits of AI are shared equitably among all members of society.

As we embrace the transformative potential of AI, we must also confront the ethical dilemmas that it presents. The development and deployment of AI must be guided by a commitment to the principles of a Gracious Society, ensuring that these technologies align with our values and work to promote empathy, compassion, and unity. To achieve this, we must foster a culture of responsible innovation, where technologists, policymakers, and citizens collaborate to shape the future of AI in a manner that reflects our shared aspirations for a Gracious Society. We must prioritize transparency, accountability, and inclusivity in the development of AI, working together to create systems that are not only powerful and efficient, but also ethical and just.

So, how do we begin this journey toward a Gracious Society powered by AI? It starts with each of us, with the choices we make and the actions we take. We must educate ourselves about the potential and pitfalls of AI, engaging in open and honest conversations about the impact of these technologies on our lives and our world. We must advocate for policies and practices that ensure the responsible development and deployment of AI, and hold ourselves and others accountable for the decisions we make.

As we stand on the brink of this new era, let us be guided by a spirit of empathy, compassion, and unity. Let us embrace the power of AI to address our most pressing challenges and build a world where everyone has the opportunity to thrive. And let us never forget that the true potential of AI lies not in the technology itself, but in our ability to use it to uplift humanity and bring us closer together than ever before.

In this spirit, I call upon each and every one of you to join me in embracing the potential of AI to foster a Gracious Society. Let us work together to ensure that this technology serves as a powerful tool for positive change, enabling us to create a world that is more just, more compassionate, and more unified. As we embark on this journey, let us be guided by the knowledge that the true power of AI lies not in its algorithms or processing capabilities, but in its capacity to bring out the best in us. For it is in harnessing this potential that we will find the inspiration and the strength to build a brighter future, a future in which AI empowers us to create a Gracious Society that reflects our highest aspirations and ensures that no one is left behind.

Thank you for being part of this important conversation. Together, we have the power to shape the course of history and redefine the role of AI in our world. Let us seize this opportunity and work together to create a Gracious Society that honors the dignity, potential, and interconnectedness of all human beings.

Part I:
The Foundations of a Gracious Society

HUMAN DIGNITY

As we continue our exploration of the Gracious Society—a society rooted in empathy, compassion, and unity—it is essential that we turn our attention to one of the foundational principles that underpin this vision: human dignity. I invite you to join me on a journey of reflection and inspiration, as we delve into the concept of human dignity and its centrality in the creation of a Gracious Society.

At its core, human dignity is the inherent worth and value that every individual possesses, simply by virtue of being human. It is a universal concept that transcends nationality, race, religion, gender, and social status, and serves as the foundation upon which our shared aspirations for justice, equality, and human rights are built. In a Gracious Society, human dignity is not only recognized but actively promoted and protected, ensuring that every person has the opportunity to live a life of meaning, purpose, and fulfillment. To understand the centrality of human dignity in a Gracious Society, we must first examine the ways in which this concept is woven into the very fabric of our existence. Human dignity is reflected in the principles of equality and non-discrimination, which affirm that every individual is entitled to the same rights, freedoms, and opportunities, regardless of their background or circumstances. It is also embodied in the notion of autonomy and self-determination, which recognizes that each person has the right to make decisions about their own life and to chart their own course in the pursuit of happiness and well-being.

In a Gracious Society, human dignity is not only acknowledged as a fundamental principle, but it is also actively nurtured and cultivated through the policies and practices that shape our communities. This involves creating inclusive spaces where every individual feels welcomed, respected, and valued, and where diverse perspectives and experiences are celebrated as integral parts of our collective identity. It also requires addressing the structural barriers and systemic inequalities that undermine human dignity and perpetuate cycles of poverty, discrimination, and marginalization.

One of the most powerful ways in which we can promote human dignity in a Gracious Society is by fostering a culture of empathy, compassion, and understanding. When we truly see one another—when we recognize the humanity and worth of every individual—we are moved to act in ways that uplift and empower those around us. By embracing empathy and compassion as core values, we can create a ripple effect that reverberates throughout our communities, our societies, and ultimately, our world.

This brings us to the role of AI in promoting human dignity within the Gracious Society. As we have discussed, AI holds tremendous potential to revolutionize various aspects of our lives, from healthcare and education to environmental conservation and beyond. But, perhaps most importantly, AI has the power to enhance our ability to recognize and uphold human dignity on a global scale. Imagine AI systems that are designed to facilitate cross-cultural communication and understanding, breaking down barriers and fostering empathy among diverse communities. Picture AI-powered tools that help us identify and address the root causes of social inequalities, enabling us to create more just and inclusive societies. Envision AI technologies that empower individuals with disabilities, ensuring that every person has the opportunity to participate fully and meaningfully in the world around them.

As we harness the potential of AI to advance human dignity within the Gracious Society, we must also be vigilant in ensuring that these technologies are developed and deployed in ways that respect and protect the dignity of every individual. This means prioritizing transparency, fairness, and accountability in the design and implementation of AI systems, and engaging in ongoing dialogues about the ethical implications of these technologies. It also means working to bridge the digital divide, ensuring that the benefits of AI are accessible to all, regardless of their socio-economic status or geographic location.

The journey toward a Gracious Society begins with a commitment to human dignity—a commitment that must be nurtured and sustained through our collective actions, values, and aspirations. As we embrace the transformative potential of AI, let us use this powerful technology as a force for good, one that promotes human dignity and paves the way for a more compassionate, inclusive, and unified world.

Together, we have the power to shape the course of history and redefine the role of AI in our society. By placing human dignity at the center of our vision for a Gracious Society, we can create a future that honors the inherent worth and value of every individual, and ensures that no one is left behind. Let us be guided by our shared commitment to empathy, compassion, and unity, and let us work together to build a world in which every person has the opportunity to live a life of dignity, purpose, and fulfillment.

It is our collective responsibility to ensure that the advancements we make in AI and technology are used to create a better world for all, a world in which human dignity is recognized, respected, and celebrated.

HUMAN DIGNITY IN PRACTICE

As we delve deeper into our exploration of the Gracious Society, we must turn our focus to the ways in which we can respect and promote human dignity in all aspects of life. I invite you to join me on a journey of inspiration and empowerment, as we examine the importance of human dignity in the fabric of our daily existence and share powerful case study examples that demonstrate the transformative potential of upholding human dignity in practice.

Human dignity, the inherent worth and value of every individual, is the cornerstone of a Gracious Society. It is a universal concept that transcends the boundaries of nationality, race, religion, gender, and social status, and serves as the foundation for our shared aspirations for justice, equality, and human rights. In a Gracious Society, human dignity is not only recognized but actively promoted and protected, ensuring that every person has the opportunity to live a life of meaning, purpose, and fulfillment.

Respecting and promoting human dignity in all aspects of life requires a multifaceted approach, encompassing the personal, social, and institutional dimensions of our existence. At the individual level, it begins with cultivating empathy and compassion, developing the capacity to understand and appreciate the experiences and perspectives of others, and recognizing our shared humanity. This involves listening deeply to the stories and voices of those around us, and taking the time to reflect on the ways in which our actions, choices, and beliefs impact the well-being and dignity of others.

At the social level, respecting and promoting human dignity entails fostering a culture of inclusivity, where every person is valued, respected, and welcomed. This means challenging stereotypes and prejudices, celebrating diversity, and working together to create communities that are characterized by understanding, trust, and solidarity. In this context, I'd like to share a powerful case study example:

Consider the story of the Homeboy Industries, an organization founded by Father Greg Boyle in Los Angeles. Homeboy Industries provides hope, training, and support to formerly gang-involved and previously incarcerated men and women, allowing them to redirect their lives and become contributing members of society. The organization embraces the principles of human dignity by offering a safe and supportive environment for individuals to heal, grow, and transform their lives. In doing so, it not only empowers these individuals but also strengthens the fabric of the community, fostering empathy, compassion, and unity. According to their website, "Each year over 10,000 former gang members from across Los Angeles come through Homeboy Industries' doors in an effort to make a positive change. They are welcomed into a community of mutual kinship, love, and a wide variety of services ranging from tattoo removal to anger management and parenting classes." I encourage each person reading this book to look at similar organizations in your community that are making lasting generational impacts and contributing your time, money or just spreading their message for the greater support of creating a Gracious Society.

At the institutional level, promoting human dignity involves the creation of policies and structures that ensure equal opportunities, social justice, and human rights for all. This requires addressing systemic inequalities and barriers that prevent individuals from realizing their full potential and participating meaningfully in society.

One notable example in this regard is the Grameen Bank, founded by Nobel Peace Prize laureate Muhammad Yunus in Bangladesh. The Grameen Bank provides microcredit to the poor, especially women, enabling them to start their own businesses and lift themselves out of poverty. By recognizing and promoting the inherent dignity and potential of each individual, the Grameen Bank has empowered millions of people to transform their lives and their communities. The primary objective of The Grameen Bank is to promote financial independence among the poor. In Muhammad Yunus' book Banker to the Poor: Micro-lending and the Battle Against World Poverty, he writes saying, "When you hold the world in your palm and inspect it only from a bird's eye view, you tend to become arrogant, you do not realize things become blurred when viewed from an enormous distance. I opted instead for the 'worms eye view'.....The poor taught me an entirely new economics. I learned about the problems they face from their own perspective."

As we continue to explore the importance of respecting and promoting human dignity in all aspects of life, we must also recognize the potential of AI and other technologies to contribute to this endeavor. By designing AI systems that respect human dignity, we can develop tools and applications that empower individuals, promote social cohesion, and address the structural barriers that perpetuate inequality and injustice.

For example, AI-driven educational platforms can help level the playing field for students from diverse backgrounds, providing personalized learning experiences that cater to each individual's unique needs and abilities. In doing so, these technologies can promote human dignity by ensuring that every child has the opportunity to reach their full potential, regardless of their socio-economic status or geographic location.

In our pursuit of a Gracious Society, it is our collective responsibility to respect and promote human dignity in all aspects of life. As we navigate the complexities and challenges of our modern world, we must remain steadfast in our commitment to empathy, compassion, and unity, and actively seek out opportunities to uplift and empower those around us. By sharing these inspiring case study examples, I hope to illustrate the transformative potential of upholding human dignity in practice. Whether through the work of organizations like Homeboy Industries and the Grameen Bank, or through the development of AI-driven educational platforms, we have the power to create a world where human dignity is recognized, respected, and celebrated in every corner of our society.

Let us remember that the journey toward a Gracious Society begins with each and every one of us. By embracing the principles of human dignity and working together to create a more just, compassionate, and inclusive world, we can ensure that no one is left behind and that every individual has the opportunity to live a life of meaning, purpose, and fulfillment. Together, let us be inspired by these powerful stories and examples, and let us work collectively to create a Gracious Society that honors the dignity, potential, and interconnectedness of all human beings.

SOLIDARITY

Let's examine the principle of solidarity, its implications for society, and the transformative potential it holds for our world. Solidarity is the spirit of unity and shared responsibility that binds us together as a global community, transcending the boundaries of nationality, race, religion, and culture. It is a principle rooted in the recognition that our fates are inextricably linked, and that the well-being of each individual is deeply connected to the well-being of all. In a Gracious Society, solidarity serves as the foundation for collective action, enabling us to address the myriad challenges we face – from poverty and inequality to climate change and beyond – with a sense of shared purpose and mutual support.

The principle of solidarity has profound implications for society, shaping the way in which we understand and engage with the world around us. When we embrace solidarity, we acknowledge our interconnectedness and commit ourselves to the pursuit of common goals, recognizing that our collective strength lies in our ability to work together in the face of adversity. Solidarity calls us to stand in support of those who are marginalized or oppressed, to amplify the voices of those who are often silenced, and to work collaboratively to create a more just, equitable, and compassionate world.

One powerful example of solidarity in action is the global response to the COVID-19 pandemic. When the pandemic struck, nations around the world united in a shared commitment to protect public health and prevent the spread of the virus. Scientists collaborated across borders to develop vaccines at an unprecedented pace, while healthcare workers put their lives on the line to care for those in need. In the face of extraordinary challenges, people around the world demonstrated an unwavering spirit of solidarity, coming together to support one another and tackle the crisis head-on.

Another inspiring instance of solidarity is the global movement for climate justice. As the devastating impacts of climate change become increasingly apparent, people from all walks of life are rallying together to demand urgent action to protect our planet and secure a sustainable future for generations to come. This movement, fueled by a powerful sense of solidarity, has succeeded in placing climate change at the forefront of the international agenda, spurring governments and businesses to adopt more ambitious climate policies and invest in clean energy technologies.

Solidarity also plays a critical role in the fight for social justice and human rights. Across the globe, individuals and organizations are standing together in support of marginalized communities, working tirelessly to promote equality and challenge discrimination in all its forms. From the Black Lives Matter movement to the struggle for LGBTQ+ rights, these campaigns are grounded in a deep commitment to solidarity and a shared belief in the power of collective action to drive meaningful change. As we continue to explore the principle of solidarity and its implications for society, it is essential that we recognize the vital role that emerging technologies, such as AI, can play in fostering solidarity and promoting a Gracious Society. By harnessing the power of AI to facilitate communication, bridge cultural divides, and empower marginalized communities, we can strengthen the bonds of solidarity that unite us and pave the way for a more just and compassionate world.

In our pursuit of a Gracious Society, the principle of solidarity serves as a beacon of hope, guiding us toward a brighter, more inclusive future. As we navigate the complexities and challenges of our modern world, let us remain steadfast in our commitment to solidarity, recognizing that our collective strength lies in our ability to work together in the face of adversity. Let us remember that the journey toward a Gracious Society begins with each and every one of us. By embracing the principles of solidarity and working together to create a more just, equitable, and compassionate world, we can ensure that no one is left behind and that every individual has the opportunity to live a life of meaning, purpose, and fulfillment.

Together, let us be inspired by the power of collective action and the transformative potential it holds for our world. Let us commit ourselves to fostering solidarity in our everyday lives, and let us work hand in hand to create a Gracious Society that honors the interconnectedness of all human beings.

As we conclude this discussion on solidarity, I encourage each of you to reflect on the ways in which you can contribute to the cultivation of a Gracious Society. Whether through small acts of kindness or large-scale initiatives, every effort to promote solidarity and unity can have a lasting impact on our world. Let us move forward with a renewed sense of purpose and a shared commitment to creating a future that is defined by empathy, compassion, and solidarity.

EXAMPLES OF SOLIDARITY

In our previous discussions, we explored the principle of solidarity and its implications for society. Now, I invite you to join me on a journey of inspiration, as we examine real-life examples of solidarity in action, focusing on the inspiring work of organizations that embody this transformative principle. Solidarity is the lifeblood of a Gracious Society, the force that binds us together as we work toward common goals and shared aspirations. As we consider these case study examples, I hope you will be inspired by the incredible power of solidarity to break down barriers, overcome challenges, and pave the way for a more just, equitable, and compassionate world.

Doctors Without Borders (Médecins Sans Frontières)

Our first example of an organization exemplifying solidarity in action is Doctors Without Borders, also known as Médecins Sans Frontières (MSF). MSF is an international humanitarian organization that provides medical assistance to people affected by conflict, epidemics, disasters, or exclusion from healthcare. With a spirit of solidarity at its core, MSF sends medical professionals to the front lines of crises, offering life-saving care to those in need, regardless of their race, religion, or political affiliation. By transcending national boundaries and working together in the face of adversity, MSF demonstrates the transformative power of solidarity, offering hope and healing to the world's most vulnerable populations.

The Red Cross and Red Crescent Movement

Another inspiring example of solidarity in action is the global network of the Red Cross and Red Crescent Movement. This humanitarian organization is dedicated to providing assistance, disaster relief, and education to those in need, guided by the principles of humanity, impartiality, neutrality, independence, voluntary service, unity, and universality. Through their vast network of volunteers and staff, the Red Cross and Red Crescent Movement work tirelessly to alleviate suffering and protect human dignity, embodying the spirit of solidarity that lies at the heart of a Gracious Society.

Amnesty International

Next, let us turn our attention to Amnesty International, a global human rights organization committed to fighting injustice and promoting human rights worldwide. With millions of supporters and activists, Amnesty International harnesses the power of solidarity to shed light on human rights abuses and mobilize public pressure to bring about change. By standing together in support of marginalized communities, Amnesty International demonstrates the potential of solidarity to transform the world and create a more just and equitable society.

Oxfam International

Lastly, let us consider the inspiring work of Oxfam International, a global movement of organizations working together to combat poverty, inequality, and injustice. Through advocacy, policy research, and direct assistance, Oxfam works to empower communities and promote lasting solutions to the root causes of poverty. In their pursuit of a more equitable world, Oxfam exemplifies the spirit of solidarity, uniting people from diverse backgrounds and cultures to work collaboratively towards a common goal.

As we reflect on these powerful examples of organizations embodying solidarity in action, let us be reminded of our shared responsibility to cultivate and nurture the spirit of solidarity within our own lives and communities. In our pursuit of a Gracious Society, it is up to each of us to stand together in support of our fellow human beings, recognizing that our collective strength lies in our ability to work together in the face of adversity. Let us take inspiration from the work of these remarkable organizations and their unwavering commitment to solidarity. As we continue on our journey toward a Gracious Society, let us remember that it is through acts of solidarity – both large and small – that we can forge a brighter, more inclusive future for all.

SUBSIDIARITY AND EMPOWERMENT

Having discussed the importance of solidarity and its role in uniting us, we now turn our attention to the concept of subsidiarity, a principle that encourages the empowerment of individuals and communities. Subsidiarity is the idea that decisions should be made at the most local level possible, allowing individuals and communities to take ownership of their lives and shape their own destinies. In the context of a Gracious Society, subsidiarity is a vital component, as it fosters a sense of agency, responsibility, and self-determination among people. It is through subsidiarity that we can unlock the full potential of every individual, create thriving communities, and ultimately, build a more compassionate and just world. But how can we put subsidiarity into practice, and how can it empower individuals and communities? Allow me to share some examples and insights to inspire you in our pursuit of a Gracious Society.

Decentralized decision-making and community engagement

One of the most powerful ways to promote subsidiarity is through decentralized decision-making and active community engagement. By involving local stakeholders in the decision-making process, we can ensure that the unique needs, perspectives, and aspirations of individuals and communities are taken into account. This participatory approach not only leads to more effective and responsive policies, but it also fosters a sense of ownership and responsibility among community members.

When people are given a voice and the opportunity to shape their own futures, they are more likely to invest their time, energy, and resources in the betterment of their communities. This sense of empowerment can lead to a ripple effect, inspiring others to take action and contribute to the collective well-being of their community.

Strengthening local institutions and capacity-building

Subsidiarity and empowerment go hand in hand with the strengthening of local institutions and capacity-building. By investing in the development of local organizations, we can create a strong foundation for communities to thrive and become self-sufficient. Capacity-building initiatives can take many forms, from training local leaders and providing educational resources to supporting small businesses and promoting economic development. When we empower communities with the tools and resources they need to succeed, we create an environment where individuals can flourish and contribute to the common good.

Encouraging innovation and grassroots initiatives

Another important aspect of subsidiarity is its potential to foster innovation and support grassroots initiatives. When decisions are made at the local level, there is often greater flexibility and adaptability, allowing communities to develop creative solutions to the challenges they face. By encouraging and supporting grassroots initiatives, we can tap into the wealth of knowledge, skills, and passion that exists within communities. These locally-driven projects often have a deeper understanding of the unique needs and circumstances of their community, leading to more effective and sustainable outcomes.

Promoting a culture of self-reliance and resilience

Finally, subsidiarity plays a critical role in fostering a culture of self-reliance and resilience. By empowering individuals and communities to take charge of their own lives, we cultivate a mindset of resourcefulness, adaptability, and determination. In a world that is constantly changing and facing unprecedented challenges, this resilience is invaluable. Empowered communities are better equipped to navigate adversity, overcome obstacles, and emerge stronger in the face of hardship.

As we consider the importance of subsidiarity and its potential to empower individuals and communities, let us remember that the Gracious Society is built upon the collective efforts and contributions of all its members. By embracing the principles of subsidiarity and empowerment, we can create a world where every individual has the opportunity to realize their full potential and contribute to the common good. Let us be inspired by the transformative power of subsidiarity and the potential it holds for empowering individuals and communities. As we continue our journey towards a Gracious Society, let us commit ourselves to fostering a culture of self-reliance, resilience, and shared responsibility. Together, we can create a world where every person has the opportunity to thrive, and where the collective strength of our communities serves as the foundation for a more compassionate, just, and equitable future.

EXAMPLES OF SUBSIDIARITY AND EMPOWERMENT

As we've previously discussed, subsidiarity and empowerment are essential elements in building a Gracious Society. Now, let us delve into real-life examples that demonstrate the transformative power of subsidiarity and how it can strengthen communities and unlock the potential of every individual.

Participatory Budgeting

The first inspiring example of subsidiarity in practice comes from the realm of governance and public policy: participatory budgeting. This innovative approach to public finance originated in Brazil and has since spread around the world. Participatory budgeting allows citizens to have a direct say in how a portion of the municipal budget is allocated, empowering local communities to shape their own development priorities.

This approach exemplifies subsidiarity by giving decision-making power to the local level and engaging citizens in the governance process. Through participatory budgeting, communities can prioritize their unique needs and aspirations, creating more effective and responsive policies that reflect the will of the people.

The Transition Town Movement

Our second case study is the Transition Town Movement, a grassroots initiative that began in the United Kingdom and has since spread globally. The movement focuses on building community resilience and self-sufficiency in the face of economic, social, and environmental challenges. Transition Towns emphasize subsidiarity by empowering local communities to develop their own strategies for addressing issues such as climate change, resource depletion, and economic instability. By harnessing the collective wisdom, skills, and creativity of local residents, Transition Towns demonstrate the power of subsidiarity to inspire change from the ground up.

The Mondragon Corporation

Finally, let us turn our attention to the Mondragon Corporation, a federation of worker cooperatives based in the Basque region of Spain. The Mondragon Corporation is one of the largest and most successful examples of worker-owned businesses, employing over 75,000 people across a wide range of industries.

The Mondragon model embodies subsidiarity by giving decision-making power to the workers themselves, fostering a sense of ownership, and promoting shared prosperity. By prioritizing the needs of the local community and empowering its members to shape their own economic future, the Mondragon Corporation demonstrates how subsidiarity can create a more equitable and sustainable economy.

As we reflect on these inspiring case studies of subsidiarity in practice, let us be reminded of the transformative potential that lies within each of us and our communities. When we embrace the principles of subsidiarity and empowerment, we can unlock the full potential of every individual and create a world where the collective strength of our communities serves as the foundation for a more compassionate, just, and equitable future.

Let us carry these inspiring examples in our hearts and minds as we continue on our journey toward a Gracious Society. Together, through the power of subsidiarity and empowerment, we can create a world where every person has the opportunity to thrive and contribute to the common good.

THE COMMON GOOD

We've examined the importance of human dignity, solidarity, and subsidiarity, and now we turn our attention to the fourth crucial element: the common good. The common good is a concept that transcends individual interests and encourages us to consider the well-being of society as a whole. It asks us to look beyond our own needs and desires and work together to create a world that benefits everyone. We'll delve into the meaning of the common good and explore how we can pursue it to create a more compassionate, just, and equitable society.

Defining the Common Good

At its core, the common good is about recognizing that we are all interconnected and interdependent, and that our collective well-being is inextricably linked to the well-being of each individual. It is about creating an environment where everyone has the opportunity to flourish and contribute to society, where resources are shared equitably, and where the rights and dignity of all are respected. In pursuing the common good, we must balance the needs and interests of individuals with the broader needs of the community, ensuring that no one is left behind. This requires empathy, compassion, and a commitment to working together for the benefit of all.

Pursuing the Common Good

To effectively pursue the common good, we must engage in collective action and collaboration. This involves building strong relationships and partnerships, fostering open dialogue and communication, and working together to identify and address the challenges facing our society. In our pursuit of the common good, we must also be guided by a commitment to social justice, environmental sustainability, and economic equity. By prioritizing these values, we can create a world where everyone has the opportunity to thrive and where the common good is truly realized.

Education and the Common Good

One critical avenue for pursuing the common good is education. By providing access to quality education for all, we empower individuals with the knowledge, skills, and values necessary to contribute to society and create positive change. Education is not only a fundamental human right, but it is also a cornerstone of a flourishing society, as it enables personal growth, fosters understanding and tolerance, and nurtures the leaders of tomorrow.

Healthcare and the Common Good

Another essential aspect of pursuing the common good is ensuring access to quality healthcare for all. When individuals are healthy, they are better able to fulfill their potential and contribute to society. By investing in public health and addressing the root causes of health disparities, we can create a society where everyone has the opportunity to lead healthy, fulfilling lives.

Environmental Stewardship and the Common Good

Our environment plays a critical role in our collective well-being, and environmental stewardship is a key component of the common good. By protecting our natural resources, addressing climate change, and promoting sustainable practices, we ensure a healthy planet for future generations. Environmental stewardship requires collaboration, innovation, and a commitment to the long-term well-being of both people and the planet.

Building Inclusive Communities

Finally, in pursuing the common good, we must strive to build inclusive communities where everyone feels valued and respected. This means addressing systemic injustices and working to create a more equitable society where all can thrive. It requires us to challenge our biases, embrace diversity, and cultivate a spirit of empathy and understanding.

The common good is a powerful and inspiring principle that guides us toward a more compassionate, just, and equitable world. By prioritizing the well-being of all members of society, we can build a Gracious Society that is truly grounded in the values of human dignity, solidarity, subsidiarity, and the common good.

POLICIES AND PRACTICES

Let's focus on the policies and practices that promote the well-being of all, sharing inspiring case studies of organizations that embody this principle.

Universal Basic Income

Universal Basic Income (UBI) is a policy that guarantees a minimum income to all citizens, regardless of their employment status. The idea behind UBI is to provide a financial safety net, allowing individuals to pursue education, entrepreneurship, or other opportunities that contribute to personal and societal well-being. One inspiring case study is the Finnish UBI experiment, where participants experienced improvements in well-being, mental health, and trust in society.

Accessible Healthcare

Accessible healthcare is essential for the common good. By providing affordable and quality healthcare to all citizens, we ensure that everyone has the opportunity to lead healthy, fulfilling lives. One organization that exemplifies this principle is the National Health Service (NHS) in the United Kingdom. By offering comprehensive healthcare services to all UK residents, the NHS contributes to the common good by promoting health equity and social cohesion.

Quality Education for All

Education is a cornerstone of the common good, as it empowers individuals with the knowledge and skills necessary to contribute to society. The United Nations' Sustainable Development Goal 4 focuses on ensuring inclusive and equitable quality education for all. The Malala Fund, founded by Nobel laureate Malala Yousafzai, works to ensure that every girl has access to 12 years of free, quality education. By advocating for girls' education and investing in local education initiatives, the Malala Fund helps promote the common good.

Environmental Stewardship

Protecting our environment and promoting sustainable practices are essential for the well-being of all. Organizations such as the World Wildlife Fund (WWF) work to conserve natural resources and address climate change, contributing to the common good by ensuring a healthy planet for future generations. Through innovative partnerships and policy advocacy, WWF demonstrates that collaborative action can have a significant impact on environmental stewardship.

Inclusive Workplaces

Promoting inclusive workplaces that value diversity and provide equal opportunities for all is a powerful way to contribute to the common good. Companies like Salesforce, with their commitment to equal pay, diversity, and inclusion, set an inspiring example for other organizations. By prioritizing fairness and opportunity in the workplace, Salesforce fosters a culture that supports the well-being of its employees and the broader community.

Supporting Mental Health

Mental health is a critical aspect of well-being, and policies and practices that promote mental health contribute to the common good. Organizations like the National Alliance on Mental Illness (NAMI) work to provide support, education, and advocacy for individuals and families affected by mental health conditions. Through their efforts, NAMI helps break down stigma and create a society where mental health is valued and supported.

Investing in Local Communities

Investing in local communities is a powerful way to promote the common good. Organizations like the Kiva, a microfinance platform, enable individuals and businesses to invest in the success of entrepreneurs around the world, fostering economic growth and well-being. By providing access to capital and resources, Kiva empowers people to create sustainable livelihoods and contribute to their communities.

The common good is a powerful and inspiring principle that guides us toward a more compassionate, just, and equitable world. By prioritizing the well-being of all members of society, we can build a Gracious Society that is truly grounded in the values of human dignity, solidarity, subsidiarity, and the common good. The policies and practices we've discussed today, along with the inspiring case studies of organizations dedicated to these principles, serve as a testament to the incredible potential that lies within our collective efforts. Let us carry this vision forward, embracing the spirit of collaboration, empathy, and innovation, to create a better world for ourselves and future generations.

THE PREFERENTIAL OPTION FOR THE POOR

We have discussed human dignity, solidarity, subsidiarity, and the common good, and now we arrive at the fifth vital element: the preferential option for the poor. We will explore the significance of prioritizing the needs of the poor and vulnerable in our pursuit of a truly gracious society. When we speak of the preferential option for the poor, we refer to a moral imperative that calls us to prioritize the needs of the most vulnerable and marginalized members of our society. This principle, deeply rooted in the social teachings of various faiths and humanist philosophies, compels us to recognize that our collective well-being depends on the well-being of every individual, especially those who are most often left behind.

Why is it so important to prioritize the needs of the poor and vulnerable? Let's consider a few key reasons.

Intrinsic Human Dignity

First and foremost, we must remember that every human being possesses intrinsic dignity and worth. As such, the well-being of each person, regardless of their socioeconomic status or background, is of equal importance. By embracing the preferential option for the poor, we affirm our commitment to the dignity of every individual and ensure that no one is left behind in our pursuit of a more just and equitable world.

Building a Strong Foundation for Society

A society that prioritizes the needs of the poor and vulnerable is one that is built on a strong foundation. By addressing the root causes of poverty and inequality, we can create a more stable and resilient society, in which everyone can thrive. This not only benefits the poor and marginalized but also contributes to the overall health and prosperity of the entire community.

Fostering Social Cohesion and Empathy

Prioritizing the needs of the poor and vulnerable also fosters social cohesion and empathy. When we recognize the interconnectedness of our well-being and work together to uplift those who are struggling, we cultivate a spirit of compassion and solidarity. This sense of unity and shared purpose is essential to the creation of a truly gracious society.

Unleashing Human Potential

Lastly, the preferential option for the poor is critical to unleashing the full potential of every individual. When we invest in the well-being of the most vulnerable, we empower them to contribute their unique gifts, talents, and perspectives to our collective growth and progress. By creating a society in which everyone has the opportunity to thrive, we unlock the tremendous potential that lies within each of us.

To illustrate the impact of the preferential option for the poor in action, let us consider a few inspiring examples:

The Bill and Melinda Gates Foundation

The Bill and Melinda Gates Foundation is a leading philanthropic organization that focuses on improving the quality of life for individuals around the world. They have made significant contributions to global health, education, and poverty alleviation initiatives, with a particular focus on the needs of the most vulnerable populations. By prioritizing the well-being of the poor and marginalized, the foundation has helped to drive progress and innovation in the fight against poverty, disease, and inequality.

Feeding America

Feeding America is a nationwide network of food banks and meal programs in the United States that addresses the issue of hunger among the poor and vulnerable. Through its extensive efforts, Feeding America not only provides essential sustenance to millions of people but also advocates for policies and practices that alleviate the root causes of hunger and poverty.

Heifer International

Heifer International is a global nonprofit organization that works to eradicate poverty and hunger by providing livestock, resources, and training to struggling communities. Through their holistic approach to sustainable development, Heifer International helps families become self-reliant, fostering economic growth and social empowerment in some of the world's most impoverished regions.

Ashoka

Ashoka is an international organization that supports social entrepreneurs who are creating innovative solutions to society's most pressing challenges. By providing financial support, mentorship, and access to a global network, Ashoka enables these change-makers to scale their impact and improve the lives of the poor and vulnerable around the world.

One Acre Fund

One Acre Fund is a nonprofit organization that supports smallholder farmers in Africa by providing them with the tools, resources, and training they need to increase their agricultural productivity and income. By prioritizing the needs of some of the world's poorest populations, One Acre Fund helps to combat hunger and poverty while promoting sustainable agricultural practices and rural development.

Habitat for Humanity

Habitat for Humanity is an international nonprofit organization that focuses on providing affordable housing for families in need. With the help of volunteers, donors, and partner organizations, Habitat for Humanity constructs, rehabilitates, and preserves homes around the world. By addressing the urgent need for safe, stable, and affordable housing, Habitat for Humanity works to empower low-income families and break the cycle of poverty.

One inspiring case study is the Habitat for Humanity's work in the aftermath of Hurricane Katrina in the United States. In 2005, the hurricane devastated the Gulf Coast region, leaving thousands of families homeless and struggling to rebuild their lives. Habitat for Humanity mobilized an extensive rebuilding effort, engaging volunteers from across the country to construct new homes for those affected by the disaster.

Through the "Musicians' Village" project in New Orleans, Habitat for Humanity, in collaboration with local musicians and other partners, created a vibrant, sustainable community for displaced musicians and their families. This project not only provided much-needed housing but also helped to revitalize the local cultural scene, which is essential for the city's recovery and future growth.

By prioritizing the needs of the most vulnerable and focusing on long-term solutions to the housing crisis, Habitat for Humanity plays a vital role in fostering a more gracious society where everyone has a decent place to call home. Their work demonstrates the impact that compassionate action and community engagement can have on the lives of those in need.

These inspiring examples demonstrate the transformative power of prioritizing the needs of the poor and vulnerable. By embracing the preferential option for the poor, we can work together to create a more just, equitable, and compassionate world—a world that is truly reflective of the Gracious Society we envision.

The preferential option for the poor is an essential principle that guides us in our pursuit of a Gracious Society. It reminds us of our shared responsibility to uplift those who are struggling and to ensure that no one is left behind in our quest for a better world. By centering the needs of the most vulnerable and marginalized, we can create a more compassionate, just, and equitable society that benefits everyone. So let us carry this principle forward and let it inspire our actions, as we work together to build a truly Gracious Society for all.

PART II
AI TECHNOLOGY AND ITS ROLE IN A GRACIOUS SOCIETY

AI FOR SOCIAL GOOD

Let's talk about an incredibly powerful tool that has the potential to reshape our world for the better - artificial intelligence. AI technology has advanced rapidly in recent years, and while it's often associated with self-driving cars, virtual assistants, and other consumer technologies, there is a whole other side to AI that is making a real difference in addressing social and environmental challenges. I want to share with you some inspiring examples of AI projects that are tackling these issues head-on and are contributing to the creation of a more gracious society.

Imagine a world where we can predict and prevent the spread of infectious diseases, saving millions of lives every year. This is precisely what the team at BlueDot, a Canadian start-up, is working towards. They've developed an AI-driven platform that scans and analyzes vast amounts of data from sources like news reports, airline ticketing, and animal disease networks to identify potential outbreaks of infectious diseases. By providing early warning to governments, public health organizations, and hospitals, BlueDot is helping to prevent pandemics before they happen and protect vulnerable populations.

Let's talk about another pressing global issue: climate change. The Climate AI project, led by researchers at Stanford University, aims to leverage AI technologies to tackle the complex challenges of climate change. They're using advanced machine learning algorithms to optimize renewable energy generation, improve climate models, and develop more efficient carbon capture technologies. Their work promises to accelerate the transition to a more sustainable future and help mitigate the devastating effects of climate change on our planet and its inhabitants.

Education is a critical aspect of human development and a cornerstone of a gracious society. Unfortunately, millions of children around the world still lack access to quality education. That's where AI comes in. An organization called Onebillion has created an AI-driven learning platform called "onetabletperchild" to help children in developing countries learn to read, write, and do arithmetic. By adapting to each child's learning pace and providing personalized feedback, the platform empowers students to take control of their education and unlocks their potential for growth and success.

Now, imagine a world where natural disasters no longer catch us off guard, and we can better prepare for and respond to them. AI has the potential to make this a reality. For instance, the AI for Disaster Response (AIDR) project by the Qatar Computing Research Institute (QCRI) uses machine learning algorithms to analyze social media data during natural disasters. It provides real-time, actionable information to emergency responders, helping them make more informed decisions and save lives during these critical moments.

Lastly, let's talk about the power of AI to promote inclusivity and accessibility. The Seeing AI app, developed by Microsoft, is designed to help visually impaired people better navigate the world around them. By using AI algorithms to recognize and describe objects, people, and text, the app serves as a powerful tool for visually impaired individuals, enabling them to live more independently and participate more fully in society.

These are just a few examples of the incredible potential of AI technology to address social and environmental challenges. By harnessing the power of artificial intelligence, we can create innovative solutions to some of the most pressing issues facing our world today. As we continue to explore the capabilities of AI, it's essential that we keep our focus on projects that align with the values of a gracious society - empathy, compassion, unity, and a commitment to the well-being of all.

AI technology has the potential to revolutionize our efforts to create a more gracious society. From predicting disease outbreaks and combating climate change to empowering children with education and promoting accessibility, AI is helping us tackle the most pressing challenges of our time. As we continue to develop and deploy AI technologies, let us remember the potential they hold for creating a better, more just world and strive to ensure that they are harnessed for the greater good. By focusing on AI for social good, we have an unprecedented opportunity to reshape our society, tackle global challenges, and ultimately foster a world that is more gracious, compassionate, and inclusive.

AI IN HEALTHCARE

Let's discuss a topic that touches the lives of each and every one of us: healthcare. The way we approach healthcare has the power to shape our society, and today, I want to share with you an emerging force that holds the potential to revolutionize this vital sector - artificial intelligence. More specifically, I'd like to explore the incredible promise AI holds in predicting diseases and personalizing treatments, ultimately leading to a more gracious and compassionate society. Imagine a world where diseases are no longer a death sentence or a lifelong struggle, but rather, a challenge that can be anticipated, treated, and overcome with the help of AI. This vision is not a far-fetched dream; it's a reality that is slowly taking shape before our very eyes.

One of the most exciting applications of AI in healthcare is its potential to predict diseases before they even manifest. By analyzing vast amounts of patient data, AI algorithms can identify patterns and risk factors that may indicate the onset of a disease. This early warning system can empower doctors and patients to take proactive measures to prevent or mitigate the impact of these illnesses.

For instance, Google's DeepMind has developed an AI system capable of detecting early signs of diabetic retinopathy and age-related macular degeneration, two leading causes of blindness worldwide. By scanning retinal images, the AI can identify signs of these diseases with an accuracy that rivals human experts, allowing for earlier intervention and potentially saving millions of people from losing their sight.

Now, let's discuss the power of AI in personalizing treatments. Each of us is unique, and our bodies respond differently to various treatments. AI has the potential to analyze our genetic makeup, lifestyle factors, and medical history to develop highly personalized treatment plans that maximize our chances of recovery and minimize side effects.

Take the case of cancer treatment, for example. Traditionally, cancer patients often undergo a one-size-fits-all approach, involving aggressive chemotherapy or radiation therapy, which can cause significant side effects and may not even be effective for certain patients. AI has the potential to change this. By analyzing the genetic makeup of a tumor, AI systems can identify the most effective treatment options for each individual patient, increasing the likelihood of successful outcomes and reducing the burden of side effects.

IBM's Watson for Oncology is one such AI platform that is already transforming cancer care. By analyzing vast amounts of medical literature, patient data, and treatment outcomes, Watson can recommend personalized treatment plans for cancer patients, taking into account their unique circumstances and needs. By leveraging the power of AI, oncologists are better equipped to make informed decisions and provide optimal care for their patients.

The potential of AI in healthcare is not limited to predicting diseases and personalizing treatments. AI can also improve the efficiency of healthcare systems, reduce costs, and enhance patient experiences. For example, AI-driven chatbots can provide medical advice and triage patients, helping to reduce the strain on overburdened healthcare systems. AI can also be used to optimize hospital workflows, ensuring that resources are allocated effectively and that patients receive timely care.

The potential of AI in predicting diseases and personalizing treatments is nothing short of groundbreaking. As we continue to develop and deploy AI technologies in healthcare, we have the opportunity to create a more gracious society, where healthcare is tailored to individual needs, diseases are caught and treated early, and the well-being of every person is prioritized.

AI HEALTHCARE: ETHICAL CONSIDERATIONS

As we strive to create a gracious society, it is crucial that we carefully consider the ethical implications of using AI in healthcare and its impact on human dignity. In this talk, I will delve into some of the key ethical considerations that must be addressed to ensure a compassionate, just, and inclusive future.

First and foremost, we must consider the importance of privacy and data protection. AI systems in healthcare rely on vast amounts of sensitive patient data to function effectively. This data can include medical records, genetic information, and lifestyle habits, all of which are deeply personal and deserve the utmost protection. As we work to harness the power of AI, we must ensure that robust measures are in place to protect patient privacy and prevent unauthorized access to this sensitive information.

Furthermore, we must address the potential for bias in AI systems. AI algorithms are only as good as the data they are trained on, and if that data is biased or unrepresentative, the resulting AI system may perpetuate or even exacerbate existing disparities in healthcare. For instance, if an AI system is trained on data that predominantly consists of one demographic group, it may fail to accurately diagnose or treat individuals from other groups, leading to suboptimal care and potentially even harm. To create a truly gracious society, we must prioritize the development of diverse, representative datasets and work to minimize bias in AI systems.

Another ethical consideration is the issue of transparency and explain ability. AI systems can sometimes act as "black boxes," making decisions without providing clear explanations as to how or why they arrived at those decisions. This lack of transparency can make it difficult for healthcare providers and patients to trust AI systems and may undermine the patient-provider relationship. To maintain human dignity and ensure informed decision-making, it is essential that AI systems are designed to be transparent and explainable.

Additionally, we must consider the potential impact of AI on the healthcare workforce. While AI has the potential to improve efficiency and reduce the burden on healthcare professionals, there is also the risk of job displacement or a shift in roles and responsibilities. As we work towards a gracious society, it is our responsibility to ensure that healthcare professionals are equipped with the necessary skills and knowledge to adapt to the changing landscape and continue to provide high-quality, compassionate care.

Lastly, we must not forget the importance of human connection in healthcare. While AI systems can analyze data, predict outcomes, and recommend treatments, they cannot replace the empathy, compassion, and understanding that only a human healthcare provider can offer. As we integrate AI into healthcare, it is crucial that we preserve the human element and continue to prioritize the patient-provider relationship.

The potential of AI in healthcare is immense, but it also presents a range of ethical considerations that must be addressed to ensure a gracious society. By carefully considering the impact of AI on privacy, data protection, bias, transparency, workforce, and human connection, we can work together to harness the power of AI while preserving human dignity and fostering a more compassionate and inclusive world.

AI EDUCATION

Let us explore the exciting intersection of artificial intelligence and education. As we strive to create a gracious society, we must recognize that education is a cornerstone of human dignity, personal growth, and societal progress. In today's rapidly changing world, it is more important than ever to ensure that every individual has the opportunity to learn and grow to their fullest potential. One of the most promising ways to achieve this is by harnessing the power of AI to create personalized learning experiences and adaptive feedback.

Imagine a world where education is not a one-size-fits-all approach, but a tailored journey that adapts to each learner's unique needs, abilities, and interests. A world where learning is not confined to the four walls of a classroom but is an ongoing, dynamic process that evolves as the learner grows. This is the vision of the future that AI can help us achieve.

AI-driven personalized learning experiences have the potential to revolutionize the way we learn and grow. By analyzing vast amounts of data on a learner's progress, interests, and learning style, AI systems can create customized learning pathways that cater to each individual's unique needs. This means that each learner is presented with the right content, at the right time, in the right format, maximizing engagement and retention.

One of the most powerful aspects of AI-driven personalized learning is its ability to provide adaptive feedback. In traditional educational settings, feedback is often limited to periodic assessments, such as tests and quizzes. However, AI can provide real-time, granular feedback on a learner's progress, allowing them to course-correct and adjust their learning strategies as needed. This ongoing feedback loop empowers learners to take charge of their own education and fosters a growth mindset.

The benefits of personalized learning experiences and adaptive feedback extend far beyond individual learners. By creating a more engaging and effective learning experience, we can help to close the achievement gap and ensure that every learner, regardless of their background or abilities, has the opportunity to succeed.

AI-driven personalized learning can help to alleviate some of the challenges faced by educators. By automating aspects of lesson planning, content delivery, and assessment, AI systems can free up teachers to focus on what they do best: inspiring and nurturing their students. This not only reduces the burden on educators but also helps to create a more collaborative and supportive learning environment.

There are already several examples of AI in education that are making a tangible impact on learners and educators alike. For instance, platforms like DreamBox and Smart Sparrow use AI-driven adaptive learning technologies to provide personalized learning experiences in subjects such as mathematics and science. These platforms have been shown to improve learning outcomes and boost student engagement, proving that the promise of AI in education is not just a distant dream but a reality that is already unfolding.

Of course, as with any technological innovation, there are important ethical considerations to bear in mind as we integrate AI into education. We must ensure that the data used to drive these personalized learning experiences is protected, and that privacy concerns are addressed. We must also be vigilant in minimizing potential biases in AI algorithms, ensuring that these systems are inclusive and equitable for all learners.

The potential of AI to create personalized learning experiences and adaptive feedback is immense, and it offers us a unique opportunity to reshape the educational landscape for the better. By harnessing the power of AI in education, we can create a more equitable, inclusive, and effective learning environment that empowers every individual to reach their fullest potential. As we work together to create a gracious society, let us embrace the possibilities that AI offers us in education, ensuring that every learner has the opportunity to grow and thrive.

AI EDUCATION: EQUAL ACCESS

As we've discussed, artificial intelligence has the potential to revolutionize the way we teach and learn, creating personalized learning experiences that cater to each individual's unique needs, abilities, and interests. However, for these transformative technologies to truly benefit everyone, we must work to bridge the digital divide and ensure that no learner is left behind. In a world where technology is increasingly shaping the future, access to AI-driven educational tools is not just a luxury; it is a necessity. It is our collective responsibility to ensure that every learner, regardless of their socio-economic background or geographic location, has the opportunity to benefit from these innovations.

We must recognize that the digital divide is not just about access to devices and connectivity, but also about the skills and support needed to harness these technologies effectively. This requires a comprehensive approach that encompasses infrastructure, training, and ongoing support for both learners and educators.

First and foremost, we must invest in the necessary infrastructure to provide affordable, high-speed internet access to every corner of the globe. This will involve collaboration between governments, businesses, and non-profit organizations to develop innovative solutions that can overcome geographical and economic barriers. From satellite-based internet service to community-driven broadband initiatives, we have the tools and the ingenuity to bridge the digital divide, but we must commit ourselves to this cause fully.

We need to provide educators with the training and support they need to effectively integrate AI-driven educational tools into their teaching practices. This involves not just technical training but also pedagogical support, helping educators to understand how to use these tools to enhance their instruction and support the diverse needs of their students. Through targeted professional development programs, peer-to-peer learning networks, and ongoing support, we can empower educators to harness the full potential of AI in education.

Moreover, we must ensure that students themselves have the skills and support they need to make the most of AI-driven educational tools. This means providing digital literacy training that goes beyond basic computer skills, equipping learners with the critical thinking and problem-solving abilities needed to navigate the digital world effectively. In addition, we must create inclusive learning environments that cater to the diverse needs of all learners, including those with disabilities and special needs.

Another critical aspect of ensuring equal access to AI-driven educational tools is to develop solutions that are affordable, scalable, and sustainable. This will require collaboration between the public and private sectors, as well as the creative use of open-source and crowd-sourced technologies. By developing AI-driven educational tools that are accessible to all, regardless of their ability to pay, we can help to democratize education and level the playing field for all learners.

There are already inspiring examples of initiatives that are working to bridge the digital divide and ensure equal access to AI-driven educational tools. One such initiative is the One Laptop per Child project, which has distributed millions of low-cost, rugged laptops to children in developing countries, providing them with access to digital learning resources and empowering them to become active participants in the digital world. Similarly, the Khan Academy, a non-profit educational organization, offers free, high-quality online learning resources in a wide range of subjects, allowing learners from all backgrounds to access world-class educational content at no cost. By harnessing the power of AI-driven personalized learning, the Khan Academy is helping to level the playing field for learners around the globe.

As we embrace the potential of AI in education, we must also recognize our responsibility to ensure that these transformative technologies benefit all learners, not just a privileged few. By investing in infrastructure, training, and support, and by developing affordable, scalable, and sustainable solutions, we can help to bridge the digital divide and create a more equitable, inclusive, and create a more equitable, inclusive, and compassionate world through education. As we stand at the dawn of a new era in education, fueled by the potential of AI-driven learning tools, it is imperative that we remain focused on creating a future where no one is left behind. We have the opportunity to harness the power of AI to drive positive change in the lives of millions of learners, and we must take this responsibility seriously.

In this journey, we must be guided by the principles of empathy, compassion, and solidarity. We must work together, as a global community, to support the development of educational solutions that address the unique challenges faced by learners in different contexts and environments. By fostering collaboration and knowledge-sharing between stakeholders in the public, private, and non-profit sectors, we can ensure that the benefits of AI-driven educational tools are felt by all.

Furthermore, we must recognize that ensuring equal access to AI-driven educational tools is not a one-time effort but an ongoing commitment. As technology evolves and new solutions emerge, we must continue to invest in the development and deployment of inclusive, accessible, and affordable educational tools that cater to the needs of all learners.

The potential of AI-driven educational tools to transform the way we learn and grow is immense, but only if we rise to the challenge of ensuring equal access for all.

AI AND ENVIRONMENTAL SUSTAINABILITY

Let's explore the critical role that artificial intelligence plays in our ongoing battle against the existential threat of environmental degradation and climate change. We stand at a pivotal moment in history, where our decisions and actions will determine the fate of our planet and the generations that follow. AI technology presents us with a remarkable opportunity to optimize resource use, monitor ecosystems, and ultimately, protect our planet.

Our world is grappling with the devastating consequences of climate change, from the loss of biodiversity to the increasing frequency of extreme weather events. It is no secret that our relentless consumption of resources and disregard for the environment has brought us to the brink of disaster. However, there is hope, and that hope lies in the power of technology, specifically the power of AI, to help us address these challenges head-on.

Imagine a world where AI algorithms analyze vast amounts of data to optimize energy consumption, reducing greenhouse gas emissions and our dependence on fossil fuels. These intelligent systems can predict and prevent equipment failures in power plants, improving efficiency and reducing waste. Furthermore, AI can be harnessed to develop advanced energy storage solutions, enabling us to capture and store renewable energy more effectively.

In agriculture, AI-powered systems can revolutionize the way we grow food, enabling us to optimize water and fertilizer use, reduce waste, and improve crop yields. By analyzing data from satellites, drones, and ground-based sensors, AI can provide farmers with real-time insights into the health of their crops and the condition of their soil, allowing them to make informed decisions about resource allocation. But the potential of AI to drive environmental sustainability goes beyond optimizing resource use. AI can also play a vital role in monitoring ecosystems, helping us to better understand and protect the delicate balance of our natural world. AI-powered systems can process vast amounts of data from satellite images, drones, and remote sensors to track deforestation, monitor the health of coral reefs, and detect illegal fishing activities.

These intelligent systems can help us identify patterns and trends that would otherwise remain hidden, enabling us to take timely and targeted action to protect vulnerable ecosystems and the countless species that depend on them. By combining AI with other advanced technologies, such as robotics and the Internet of Things, we can create interconnected networks of sensors and monitoring devices that offer unprecedented insights into the health of our planet.

The potential of AI to transform our relationship with the environment is immense, but we must remain vigilant and responsible in its development and deployment. As we harness the power of AI to address the challenges of environmental sustainability, we must also ensure that these technologies are developed and used ethically and equitably. We must work together, across borders and industries, to share knowledge, resources, and expertise. We must be guided by the principles of empathy, compassion, and solidarity, recognizing that the health of our planet is a shared responsibility that transcends national boundaries and political divides.

Let us remember that the potential of AI to drive positive change is inextricably linked to our willingness to embrace collaboration, innovation, and a relentless commitment to the common good. Our future, and the future of generations to come, depends on our ability to harness the power of AI to create a more sustainable, equitable, and gracious society.

AI CLIMATE CHANGE

Climate change is the single most significant challenge that humanity has ever faced. We have witnessed its impact in the form of wildfires, floods, and extreme weather events that disrupt ecosystems, displace communities, and threaten the very existence of countless species. It is in these perilous times that we must look to innovative solutions such as AI to help us tackle this immense challenge. When it comes to understanding and combating climate change, the power of AI is unparalleled. AI has the potential to analyze vast amounts of complex data, identify patterns and trends, and make predictions about the future that can inform our response to this global crisis. This ability to process information at an unprecedented scale can provide us with valuable insights into the mechanisms driving climate change and offer innovative strategies for mitigation and adaptation.

For instance, AI-powered climate models can help us understand how various factors, such as greenhouse gas emissions, deforestation, and ocean temperatures, contribute to climate change. These models enable us to predict the impacts of different scenarios, allowing policymakers to make informed decisions on which strategies are most likely to be effective in combating climate change. As our understanding of the climate system deepens, AI can help refine these models, providing us with increasingly accurate and actionable insights.

In addition to improving our understanding of climate change, AI also has the potential to revolutionize our approach to mitigation and adaptation. For example, AI can optimize renewable energy production by predicting weather patterns and making real-time adjustments to solar and wind power generation. This increased efficiency can help to reduce our reliance on fossil fuels and accelerate the transition to a low-carbon economy.

AI can also play a vital role in promoting energy efficiency and reducing greenhouse gas emissions in industries such as transportation, manufacturing, and agriculture. Autonomous vehicles powered by AI can optimize traffic flow, reducing congestion and emissions. In manufacturing, AI can monitor and optimize energy use in factories, identifying inefficiencies and reducing waste. In agriculture, AI can be harnessed to develop precision farming techniques that minimize resource consumption and environmental impact.

When it comes to adaptation, AI can help us identify and respond to the impacts of climate change more effectively. For example, AI algorithms can be used to analyze satellite images and other data sources to monitor and predict the spread of wildfires, floods, and other natural disasters. By providing early warnings and real-time updates, AI can help communities prepare for and respond to these events, minimizing damage and saving lives.

AI can also be harnessed to develop innovative solutions for managing water resources, which are increasingly under threat due to climate change. By predicting demand and optimizing distribution, AI can help ensure that water is allocated efficiently and equitably, reducing waste and promoting resilience in the face of a changing climate.

The potential of AI to help us understand, mitigate, and adapt to climate change is immense, but it is essential to remember that technology alone cannot solve this problem. We must also work together, as a global community, to reduce emissions, protect vulnerable ecosystems, and promote social and economic resilience in the face of climate change. As we forge ahead in our quest to harness the power of AI to address climate change, let us remember that the success of this endeavor depends on our ability to collaborate, innovate, and maintain an unwavering commitment to the common good. This is not just a challenge for scientists, technologists, or policymakers – it is a challenge for all of us, as citizens of this planet.

ETHICAL AI DEVELOPMENT

As artificial intelligence continues to evolve and play a more significant role in our lives, it becomes crucial that we consider the ethical implications of this powerful technology. To ensure that AI is a force for good, we must address three essential principles: fairness, transparency, and accountability.

First and foremost, we must consider the importance of fairness. AI systems are only as fair as the data and algorithms that power them. As these systems become more sophisticated and integrated into various aspects of society, we must be vigilant in ensuring that they do not inadvertently perpetuate or exacerbate existing inequalities. We must ask ourselves: Does the AI system treat everyone equitably? Is the data used to train the system representative of the population it serves? Are there unintended biases in the system that may lead to discrimination or exclusion?

To achieve fairness in AI, we must adopt a proactive approach to identifying and addressing bias. This involves not only carefully curating the data used to train AI systems but also developing algorithms that actively mitigate biases that may emerge during the learning process. By doing so, we can ensure that AI technologies empower and serve all members of society, fostering a more inclusive and gracious world.

Transparency is the second critical principle in ethical AI development. As AI systems become more complex, it can be challenging to understand the logic behind their decision-making processes. This "black box" problem can lead to a lack of trust and confidence in AI technologies, which in turn can undermine their potential to benefit society. To ensure that AI serves the common good, we must strive for transparency in AI development. Transparent AI systems enable users to understand the rationale behind their decisions, fostering trust and promoting accountability. By developing AI systems with explainable, interpretable, and transparent algorithms, we can ensure that users are informed and empowered to engage with AI technologies responsibly. Furthermore, transparency in AI development helps policymakers and regulators make informed decisions about the appropriate use and governance of AI technologies, ensuring that they are harnessed for the benefit of all.

Finally, we must consider the principle of accountability in ethical AI development. As AI systems become more autonomous and capable of making decisions that have significant consequences for individuals and society, it is vital that we establish mechanisms for holding developers, operators, and users of AI technologies accountable for their actions. This involves not only creating regulatory frameworks and legal structures that govern AI development and use, but also fostering a culture of responsibility and ethical reflection among AI developers, users, and stakeholders.

Accountability in AI development means ensuring that those who create, deploy, and use AI technologies are aware of the ethical implications of their work and are committed to mitigating any potential harm. By fostering a sense of responsibility and ethical reflection, we can ensure that AI technologies are developed and used in ways that prioritize the common good and promote a gracious society.

The development of ethical AI is not merely an academic exercise or a technical challenge; it is a moral imperative. As we continue to integrate AI into every aspect of our lives, we must be vigilant in ensuring that these technologies are developed and used ethically, responsibly, and for the benefit of all. By prioritizing fairness, transparency, and accountability in AI development, we can harness the power of this transformative technology to build a more equitable, inclusive, and gracious society. But we must also recognize that the ethical development of AI is a shared responsibility. It falls not only on the shoulders of developers and policymakers but on all of us as users, citizens, and members of the human family.

Together, we can shape the future of AI and create a world where technology serves not only the privileged few but every individual, regardless of race, gender, or socioeconomic background. A world where AI is a tool for empowerment, rather than exclusion, and where technology is harnessed to address our most pressing challenges and promote the common good.

In order to achieve this vision, we must also invest in education and public awareness. By educating our societies about the ethical implications of AI and fostering critical thinking and informed decision-making, we can ensure that everyone has a voice in shaping the future of AI development. This involves creating educational programs, fostering public dialogue, and promoting media literacy to ensure that our societies are equipped to navigate the complex ethical landscape of AI and make informed choices about its use and governance.

Moreover, we must recognize the importance of multidisciplinary collaboration in the development of ethical AI. By bringing together experts from diverse fields such as computer science, philosophy, law, and social sciences, we can foster a holistic approach to AI ethics that considers not only the technical aspects of AI development but also its broader social, economic, and cultural implications.

Additionally, we must acknowledge the role of international collaboration in promoting ethical AI development.

As AI technologies transcend national boundaries and impact societies around the globe, it is crucial that we work together to establish shared principles and guidelines for ethical AI development. By fostering dialogue and cooperation among nations, we can ensure that the benefits of AI are realized globally and that the challenges and risks associated with this technology are addressed collectively. The development of ethical AI is both a challenge and an opportunity. By addressing the principles of fairness, transparency, and accountability in AI development, we can create a more gracious society where technology serves the common good, empowers individuals and communities, and helps us to tackle the most pressing challenges of our time. But this vision can only be realized if we work together, embracing our shared responsibility and commitment to the ethical development of AI.

Let us seize this opportunity to shape the future of AI and create a world where technology serves not as a force of division, but as a catalyst for unity, compassion, and human flourishing. Let us strive for a gracious society in which AI is developed and used ethically, responsibly, and for the benefit of all.

AI AND JOB OPPORTUNITIES

We will explore an issue that is at the forefront of many minds as we continue to integrate artificial intelligence into our lives: the balance between automation and the creation of new job opportunities. It's a topic that is vital to fostering a gracious society, one that values human dignity, solidarity, and the common good. The rapid advancement of AI technologies has led to concerns about job displacement and the future of work. It's true that automation has the potential to replace many jobs, particularly those that are repetitive or involve routine tasks. However, it's important to remember that the development of AI also presents us with an opportunity to reimagine the future of work, creating new job opportunities and avenues for human creativity and innovation.

As AI systems continue to evolve and become more sophisticated, we will undoubtedly see a shift in the nature of work. Rather than simply replacing jobs, AI has the potential to augment human capabilities, enhancing our productivity and allowing us to focus on higher-level tasks that require creativity, problem-solving, and empathy.

To achieve this balance, we must first understand the true impact of AI on the job market. Research conducted by the World Economic Forum suggests that, by 2025, automation will displace approximately 85 million jobs, while simultaneously creating 97 million new job opportunities. This underscores the need for a proactive approach to managing the transition and ensuring that workers have the skills and resources necessary to succeed in this new landscape.

One key strategy for balancing automation with job creation is to invest in education and workforce development. By providing individuals with access to high-quality education, training programs, and lifelong learning opportunities, we can equip them with the skills and knowledge necessary to adapt to the changing job market and thrive in the age of AI. This includes not only technical skills, such as programming and data analysis, but also soft skills, such as critical thinking, collaboration, and emotional intelligence. These skills will be in high demand as AI systems increasingly take on routine tasks, allowing humans to focus on more complex and creative endeavors.

Another essential strategy is to encourage the development of AI applications that address pressing social and environmental challenges. By focusing on the development of AI systems that contribute to the common good, we can create meaningful job opportunities that align with our values and principles as a gracious society.

For example, AI can play a critical role in advancing healthcare, education, and environmental sustainability, areas in which human ingenuity and expertise are essential. By combining human knowledge and creativity with the power of AI, we can develop innovative solutions to the world's most pressing problems, creating new job opportunities in the process.

Finally, it's important to foster a culture of collaboration between AI developers, policymakers, business leaders, and workers. By working together, these stakeholders can identify the areas in which AI can create the most significant positive impact and develop strategies to ensure that job displacement is minimized and new opportunities are created.

One example of this collaborative approach is the concept of "AI for Good," a movement that aims to harness the power of AI to address global challenges and improve the human condition. By bringing together experts from various fields and fostering interdisciplinary collaboration, we can ensure that AI is developed and deployed in a manner that benefits all members of society, not just a select few.

The future of work in the age of AI is not a zero-sum game. Rather, it's an opportunity for us to reimagine the way we live, work, and learn, and to create new job opportunities that align with our values as a gracious society. To achieve this balance, we must invest in education and workforce development, encourage the development of AI applications that contribute to the common good, and foster collaboration among stakeholders. By doing so, we can ensure that AI becomes a force for good in our world, driving positive change and enhancing the quality of life for all members of our gracious society.

As we look to the future, we must remember that the integration of AI into our lives presents us with both challenges and opportunities. The key to navigating this complex landscape lies in our ability to adapt, innovate, and collaborate, ensuring that the benefits of AI are shared equitably and that no one is left behind.

To this end, it's essential that we continue to engage in open and honest dialogue about the impact of AI on the job market and the broader society. By fostering a culture of transparency and inclusivity, we can work together to develop policies and strategies that mitigate the risks associated with automation while maximizing the potential for positive change. In particular, we must prioritize the development of policies that support displaced workers as they transition to new job opportunities. This may include initiatives such as income support, reskilling programs, and targeted investment in sectors with high growth potential.

At the same time, we must remain vigilant in our efforts to address potential biases and inequalities that may emerge as a result of AI-driven automation. By actively promoting diversity and inclusion in AI development and deployment, we can ensure that these technologies are designed with the needs of all members of society in mind, contributing to a more equitable and just world. The potential of AI to transform our world for the better is immense. However, this potential can only be realized if we approach the integration of AI into our lives with a spirit of empathy, compassion, and solidarity. By working together to balance the risks and opportunities associated with AI-driven automation, we can create a more gracious society in which human dignity, the common good, and the well-being of all people are upheld and celebrated.

AI DRIVEN WORKFORCE

We stand on the precipice of the Fourth Industrial Revolution, we find ourselves in the midst of a significant transformation brought about by the rapid advancements in artificial intelligence. This shift has already begun to impact the job market and the workforce, and it is our responsibility to ensure that we adapt and prepare ourselves for the AI-driven world that lies ahead.

Let's discuss the importance of reskilling and upskilling programs in helping individuals and communities thrive in this new era of AI-driven automation. These programs are crucial in fostering a gracious society, where every individual has the opportunity to succeed and contribute meaningfully to our shared future. The AI revolution has the potential to bring about significant economic growth and improvements in our quality of life. However, it is also accompanied by the risk of job displacement and the widening of the skills gap. By investing in reskilling and upskilling initiatives, we can help individuals transition to new job opportunities, empowering them to adapt and excel in this rapidly changing landscape.

One inspiring example of an upskilling program is the collaboration between IBM and the P-TECH initiative. Through this partnership, IBM provides students from underprivileged backgrounds with the opportunity to gain both a high school diploma and an associate degree in a STEM field. By equipping these students with the skills required to thrive in a tech-driven world, this program helps to create a more diverse and inclusive workforce, better equipped to address the challenges and opportunities of the AI revolution.

Another example comes from the World Economic Forum's Reskilling Revolution platform, which aims to provide one billion people with better education, skills, and jobs by 2030. This initiative brings together governments, businesses, and educational institutions to create scalable, actionable solutions to the challenges posed by the AI-driven workforce.

So, what can we do to support these types of programs and help individuals successfully navigate the AI-driven job market?

First, we must foster a culture of lifelong learning. In a world where the pace of change is accelerating, the ability to adapt and learn new skills is more important than ever. By encouraging individuals to embrace continuous learning and providing them with access to high-quality educational resources, we can empower them to stay relevant and thrive in the evolving job market.

Second, we must promote collaboration between industry, government, and educational institutions. The challenges posed by the AI revolution cannot be addressed by any single entity. By fostering partnerships and promoting knowledge sharing, we can develop more effective and targeted reskilling and upskilling initiatives, tailored to the specific needs of the workforce.

Third, we must ensure equal access to educational opportunities. In our pursuit of a gracious society, we must strive to eliminate disparities in access to education and training programs. By prioritizing inclusivity and providing resources to those who need them most, we can help to create a more equitable and just world.

The AI revolution presents us with a unique opportunity to redefine the future of work and to build a more compassionate, gracious society. By embracing the potential of reskilling and upskilling programs, we can ensure that every individual has the tools and resources they need to succeed in this new era.

Together, let us commit to fostering a culture of continuous learning, promoting collaboration and inclusivity, and prioritizing the needs of the most vulnerable among us. In doing so, we can create a world in which every individual has the opportunity to flourish, contributing to the greater good and the well-being of all.

PART III
BUILDING A GRACIOUS SOCIETY IN THE ERA OF AI

FOSTERING A CULTURE OF ENCOUNTER

Let's discuss a powerful message of hope and unity in a world that is being transformed by artificial intelligence. This message comes from a visionary leader who has consistently called for dialogue, understanding, and compassion in our global society. He is none other than Pope Francis.

Pope Francis, the leader of the Catholic Church, has been a staunch advocate for a culture of encounter – a culture where people from all walks of life come together to share their experiences, learn from one another, and ultimately, build a more compassionate and gracious society. In his message, Pope Francis emphasizes the importance of breaking down the walls that divide us, of fostering genuine connections with others, and of working together to address the challenges that our world faces. As we stand on the threshold of a new era, where AI technology is reshaping the way we live, work, and interact with one another, his message is more relevant than ever.

AI has the potential to revolutionize various aspects of our lives, from healthcare and education to environmental sustainability. However, it also poses ethical and social challenges that we must address collectively. The development and deployment of AI should not be an exclusive endeavor that caters only to a privileged few; instead, it should be a collective effort that benefits everyone, regardless of their socioeconomic background, nationality, or beliefs.

Pope Francis' call for a culture of encounter provides us with a roadmap for building a gracious society in the era of AI.

Let me share with you some key principles that can guide us on this journey:

- Engage in genuine dialogue: As AI reshapes our world, we must be open to engaging in honest and respectful conversations with others, especially those who hold different opinions or come from different backgrounds. By doing so, we can foster mutual understanding, challenge our assumptions, and develop more inclusive and ethically sound AI solutions.

- Embrace empathy and compassion: In a world where AI has the potential to amplify existing inequalities and create new ones, it is essential that we approach its development and deployment with empathy and compassion. We must strive to create AI solutions that prioritize the needs of the most vulnerable and marginalized members of our society.

- Foster collaboration and cooperation: Building a gracious society in the era of AI requires the collective efforts of governments, businesses, researchers, and civil society. We must work together to develop AI solutions that are guided by ethical principles and promote the common good.

- Prioritize education and lifelong learning: As AI transforms the job market and the skills required to succeed in it, we must ensure that every individual has access to quality education and the opportunity to engage in lifelong learning. By doing so, we can empower people to adapt to the changing landscape and contribute meaningfully to our shared future.

- Celebrate diversity and inclusivity: A gracious society is one where every individual, regardless of their background, has the opportunity to thrive. As we develop and deploy AI solutions, we must strive to create inclusive technologies that respect and celebrate the diversity of our global community.

The era of AI presents us with both opportunities and challenges. By embracing Pope Francis' call for a culture of encounter, we can build a gracious society that prioritizes human dignity, solidarity, and the common good. As we work together to harness the potential of AI, let us also remember to listen to one another, to learn from our differences, and to treat each other with kindness and respect. In doing so, we can create a world where everyone has the opportunity to flourish and contribute to a brighter, more compassionate future.

STRATEGIES FOR PROMOTING A CULTURE OF ENCOUNTER

As artificial intelligence continues to permeate every facet of our lives, it is essential that we find ways to maintain and strengthen the human connections that form the foundation of our society. I'd like to share with you some strategies for promoting a culture of encounter in this rapidly evolving world. These strategies will not only help us navigate the challenges and opportunities that AI presents but also ensure that we remain grounded in our shared humanity.

Leveraging technology to facilitate human connection:

While technology has, in some ways, driven us apart, it also possesses the power to bring us closer together. By using AI and other digital tools, we can create platforms that encourage dialogue, understanding, and collaboration across cultural, geographical, and social boundaries. Video conferencing, virtual reality, and AI-enhanced language translation services can help bridge the gap between individuals from diverse backgrounds, fostering empathy and connection.

Encouraging digital literacy and critical thinking:

As technology becomes more deeply ingrained in our lives, it is essential that we develop the skills necessary to navigate this digital landscape. By promoting digital literacy and critical thinking, we can empower individuals to engage with technology in a responsible and informed manner. This, in turn, will help create a more inclusive online environment that values diverse perspectives and fosters meaningful connections.

Cultivating spaces for face-to-face interaction:

While digital communication can bridge gaps between people, face-to-face interactions remain vital for building trust and understanding. It's crucial that we make an effort to create spaces and opportunities for individuals to engage with one another in person. Community centers, workshops, and local gatherings can provide the perfect environment for these encounters, fostering a culture of connection and collaboration.

Prioritizing mental health and well-being:

The rapid pace of technological advancement can often feel overwhelming, leading to feelings of isolation and disconnection. By prioritizing mental health and well-being, we can help individuals navigate these challenges and maintain meaningful connections with others. Meditation, mindfulness, and self-care practices can serve as essential tools in cultivating emotional resilience and fostering a culture of encounter.

Fostering a sense of global citizenship:

As the world becomes more interconnected through technology, it is crucial that we cultivate a sense of global citizenship. By recognizing our shared humanity and embracing our collective responsibility to one another, we can work together to address the challenges that affect us all. Encouraging cross-cultural exchange programs, global volunteer opportunities, and international collaborations can help foster this sense of unity and shared purpose.

Emphasizing the importance of empathy and compassion in AI development:

As AI continues to transform our world, we must ensure that the technology we create is grounded in empathy and compassion. By incorporating these values into the development process, we can create AI systems that prioritize human well-being and contribute to a culture of encounter. This will require collaboration between technologists, ethicists, and diverse stakeholders to create AI that truly serves humanity.

Championing ethical and responsible AI:

Finally, it is essential that we promote ethical and responsible AI development and deployment. By advocating for transparency, accountability, and fairness in AI systems, we can ensure that these technologies are used in ways that support human dignity and foster a culture of encounter. This will involve creating guidelines, regulations, and best practices that prioritize the well-being of all individuals, particularly those who are most vulnerable.

Promoting interdisciplinary collaboration:

One key strategy for fostering a culture of encounter in the era of AI is to encourage interdisciplinary collaboration. By bringing together experts from diverse fields, such as technology, sociology, psychology, and the humanities, we can create a more holistic understanding of the impact of AI on society. This will enable us to develop AI systems that are grounded in a deep understanding of human needs, values, and aspirations, thus fostering a more compassionate and inclusive world.

Educating future generations on the importance of a gracious society:

In order to build a gracious society in the era of AI, we must instill the values of empathy, compassion, and understanding in future generations. By incorporating these principles into our educational systems, we can empower our youth to become agents of positive change. Teaching children and young adults about the importance of human dignity, solidarity, and the common good will help ensure that they develop a strong foundation in these values, enabling them to contribute to the creation of a more gracious society.

Celebrating and sharing stories of encounter:

Finally, in order to foster a culture of encounter, we must celebrate and share stories of connection, understanding, and compassion. By highlighting examples of individuals and communities coming together in the face of adversity or to address common challenges, we can inspire others to follow in their footsteps. This will help create a narrative of hope, resilience, and unity that can serve as a powerful counterbalance to the forces of division and isolation that often accompany rapid technological change.

As we navigate the era of AI, it is our collective responsibility to ensure that we build a gracious society grounded in empathy, compassion, and understanding. By fostering a culture of encounter and embracing the strategies I've outlined, we can create a world in which technology serves to strengthen our shared humanity, rather than driving us apart.

As we continue to embrace these strategies, it is important to remember that building a gracious society in the era of AI is an ongoing process. We must be open to adaptation, learning, and growth as we navigate the challenges and opportunities that this rapidly changing world presents. By maintaining a focus on the values that underpin a culture of encounter, we can ensure that the advancements in AI lead to a more inclusive, compassionate, and connected global community. The era of AI presents us with both challenges and opportunities. By focusing on fostering a culture of encounter, we can ensure that the advancements in AI serve to strengthen our shared humanity, rather than driving us apart. Through collaboration, education, and a commitment to ethical and responsible AI development, we can create a gracious society that values empathy, compassion, and understanding above all else.

COLLABORATIVE EFFORTS

In our rapidly evolving world, the power of collaboration is key to harnessing the potential of AI in a way that benefits us all. Today, I would like to explore the importance of collaborative efforts among governments, NGOs, and the private sector, as we strive to create a world in which technology serves the greater good.

The power of collaboration:

At the heart of collaboration lies the understanding that no single entity can solve complex societal problems on its own. By pooling resources, expertise, and perspectives, we can achieve far more than we could individually. In the era of AI, this spirit of collaboration is crucial for ensuring that technological advancements are developed and deployed ethically and responsibly.

The role of governments:

Governments play a crucial role in the development and deployment of AI. They are responsible for creating the legal and regulatory frameworks that govern AI's use and ensure that it serves the interests of their citizens. Governments can also invest in research and development to drive innovation and create initiatives that foster collaboration between different sectors.

For example, the European Commission's "AI for People" strategy aims to create a regulatory framework that promotes the development of AI that benefits people and the environment. It also seeks to encourage collaboration between member states and stakeholders, such as researchers, businesses, and civil society organizations.

The role of NGOs:

Non-governmental organizations (NGOs) bring a wealth of expertise and passion to the table. They can act as watchdogs, holding governments and the private sector accountable for their actions. NGOs can also contribute to the development of AI solutions by providing insights into the needs of the communities they serve, ensuring that technology is developed with human-centric values in mind.

One such example is the AI for Good Foundation, which brings together AI researchers, policy experts, and humanitarian organizations to develop AI-driven solutions to global challenges, such as poverty, inequality, and environmental sustainability.

The role of the private sector:

The private sector is a driving force behind AI innovation, responsible for much of the research, development, and deployment of cutting-edge technologies. Businesses have the resources and expertise to create powerful AI solutions, but they must also be held accountable for their actions and ensure that their technologies serve the greater good.

Companies like OpenAI are working towards creating AI that is not only powerful but also safe and beneficial to humanity. By committing to research transparency, collaboration, and prioritizing long-term safety, OpenAI serves as an example of how the private sector can contribute to building a gracious society in the era of AI.

Multi-stakeholder initiatives:

One of the most effective ways to foster collaboration among governments, NGOs, and the private sector is through multi-stakeholder initiatives. These platforms bring together diverse stakeholders to work towards a common goal, such as ethical AI development, data privacy, or digital inclusion.

The Partnership on AI, for example, is a multi-stakeholder organization that aims to ensure that AI is developed and deployed in a way that benefits all of humanity. Its members include leading tech companies, academic institutions, and civil society organizations, all working together to address the global challenges posed by AI.

Overcoming barriers to collaboration:

While the benefits of collaboration are clear, it is important to acknowledge the challenges and barriers that can hinder effective cooperation. These may include competing interests, lack of trust, or cultural differences. To overcome these barriers, stakeholders must commit to open communication, transparency, and a shared vision for the future.

The importance of global cooperation:

Lastly, I want to emphasize the importance of global cooperation in building a gracious society in the era of AI. AI technologies have the potential to impact people and societies across borders, which means that their development and deployment must be approached from a global perspective. By working together on an international level, we can ensure that AI serves as a force for good, addressing the most pressing challenges facing humanity.

International frameworks and guidelines:

One way to foster global cooperation is through the development of international frameworks and guidelines that set common standards for AI development and deployment. These guidelines can provide a shared understanding of ethical principles and best practices, helping to bridge cultural, political, and economic divides.

An example of such an effort is the Organization for Economic Cooperation and Development's (OECD) AI Principles, which have been adopted by over 40 countries. These principles emphasize the importance of human-centered values, transparency, and accountability in AI development.

Sharing knowledge and resources:

Another important aspect of global cooperation is the sharing of knowledge and resources. By working together, countries can pool their expertise, data, and technological capabilities to develop AI solutions that address pressing global challenges, such as climate change, poverty, and inequality.

Initiatives like AI4D (AI for Development) bring together researchers, policymakers, and practitioners from around the world to collaborate on AI projects that promote sustainable development and social progress.

Building a global community:

Lastly, building a gracious society in the era of AI requires cultivating a global community of stakeholders who are committed to working together to address the challenges and opportunities posed by AI. This community should be inclusive and diverse, representing the full spectrum of perspectives and expertise needed to harness the potential of AI for the greater good.

Conferences, workshops, and online platforms can serve as valuable spaces for fostering dialogue and collaboration, helping to build the relationships and networks that will underpin our collective efforts to create a gracious society in the era of AI.

The era of AI presents us with both immense potential and significant challenges. If we are to build a gracious society that harnesses the power of AI for the benefit of all, collaboration among governments, NGOs, and the private sector is essential. By working together, we can ensure that AI serves as a force for good, promoting human dignity, social justice, and environmental sustainability. Let us embrace the spirit of collaboration and work together to create a world where technology truly serves humanity.

INDIVIDUAL ACTIONS

As we delve deeper into the 21st century, we find ourselves at the intersection of technological advancement and human values. As AI continues to transform our world, we must not forget the vital role each of us plays in promoting and shaping a Gracious Society. I want to discuss the power of individual action and how every single one of us can make a difference.

Embracing personal responsibility:

The first step in creating a Gracious Society is recognizing our individual responsibility. While governments, NGOs, and the private sector all play crucial roles, the ultimate driving force behind social change is the collective action of millions of individuals. Every decision we make, from the products we buy to the way we treat others, has the potential to impact our society. By becoming more conscious of the choices we make, we can begin to align our actions with our values, fostering a culture of empathy, compassion, and understanding.

Lifelong learning and critical thinking:

In a rapidly changing world, lifelong learning and critical thinking are essential skills for every individual. As AI continues to evolve, we must stay informed about the latest developments and be prepared to adapt to new technologies and paradigms. By cultivating a mindset of curiosity and continuous learning, we empower ourselves to engage in informed discussions, make responsible decisions, and contribute to the development of ethical AI solutions that serve the common good.

Engaging in dialogue:

One of the most powerful ways individuals can contribute to a Gracious Society is by engaging in dialogue. Open and respectful conversations, both online and offline, are essential for fostering understanding and bridging divides. By listening to others with empathy and sharing our own perspectives, we can challenge our assumptions, broaden our horizons, and find common ground. In this way, dialogue becomes a catalyst for social change, laying the foundation for a more inclusive and compassionate society.

Advocating for ethical AI:

As individuals, we can use our voices to advocate for ethical AI development and deployment. By raising awareness about the potential risks and benefits of AI, we can help shape public opinion and influence the decisions of policymakers, businesses, and technologists. Through writing, speaking, and engaging in public discourse, we can be champions for a Gracious Society, ensuring that AI is developed and used in ways that respect human dignity and promote social justice.

Supporting organizations and initiatives:

We also have the power to support organizations and initiatives that are working to create a Gracious Society. By volunteering our time, donating resources, or simply sharing their work with others, we can amplify their impact and help drive positive change. Whether it's a local non-profit promoting digital literacy or an international organization working on AI for social good, our support can make a real difference in the quest for a more equitable and compassionate world.

Fostering empathy and compassion:

At the heart of a Gracious Society is empathy and compassion. As individuals, we can cultivate these qualities by practicing kindness, understanding, and forgiveness in our daily lives. By treating others with respect and dignity, we can create a ripple effect that spreads throughout our communities, inspiring others to do the same. In this way, our individual actions can contribute to a larger movement, helping to build a Gracious Society where everyone has the opportunity to thrive.

Embracing diversity and inclusion:

Finally, we must embrace diversity and inclusion as essential components of a Gracious Society. As AI continues to reshape our world, we must ensure that all voices are heard, and all perspectives are taken into account. By actively seeking out and engaging with people from different backgrounds, cultures, and experiences, we can enrich our own understanding and contribute to a more inclusive and equitable society.

The power of individual action cannot be underestimated. As we navigate the complex landscape of AI and its potential impact on society, each of us has a critical role to play in building a Gracious Society. By taking personal responsibility, cultivating a love of learning, engaging in dialogue, advocating for ethical AI, supporting organizations and initiatives, fostering empathy and compassion, and embracing diversity and inclusion, we can drive meaningful change.

Remember, every action, no matter how small, has the potential to create a ripple effect that can transform our world. As the famous anthropologist Margaret Mead once said, "Never doubt that a small group of thoughtful, committed citizens can change the world; indeed, it's the only thing that ever has."

So, I invite you all to join me in this mission. Let us come together as individuals, united by a common purpose, and work towards creating a Gracious Society, where technology serves the common good, and human dignity and compassion are the foundations upon which we build our future. Together, we can harness the power of AI to enhance our world, not diminish it. We can ensure that the digital revolution is a force for good, driving progress that uplifts all of humanity.

Let us be the change we wish to see in the world. Let us be the architects of a Gracious Society that future generations will look back on with pride, knowing that we made a conscious choice to prioritize empathy, compassion, and unity in the era of AI.

WAYS TO CONTRIBUTE

Now, more than ever, we find ourselves surrounded by innovative technologies that have the potential to revolutionize every aspect of our lives. While AI brings numerous opportunities, it also presents new challenges that require our collective wisdom, empathy, and creativity.

So, how can we, as individuals, harness the power of AI to contribute to a more compassionate, inclusive world?

First, we must educate ourselves. Knowledge is power, and in the age of AI, staying informed about the latest advancements, ethical considerations, and potential implications of this technology is crucial. By understanding AI, we can engage in meaningful discussions, make informed decisions, and advocate for responsible development and deployment.

Second, we must develop empathy and compassion. AI has the potential to impact the lives of countless individuals around the world. We must remember that behind every algorithm, there are real people with unique experiences, hopes, and dreams. As we interact with AI systems, let us strive to maintain our humanity by treating others with kindness, understanding, and respect.

Third, let's embrace diversity and inclusion. AI systems are built on data that reflects the diverse experiences and perspectives of people around the world. To ensure that these technologies serve everyone equitably, we must actively seek out and include diverse voices in their development. By fostering an inclusive environment, we can create AI that is truly representative of the human experience.

Fourth, let's advocate for transparency and accountability. As AI continues to shape our world, it is crucial that we demand transparency in how these systems are designed, developed, and deployed. By holding developers, companies, and governments accountable, we can ensure that AI technologies are used ethically and responsibly, for the benefit of all.

Fifth, let's support organizations and initiatives that prioritize human dignity and the common good. By contributing our time, resources, and expertise to organizations working to promote ethical AI development, we can help ensure that these technologies are used to uplift and empower individuals, rather than marginalize and exploit them.

Sixth, let's engage in dialogue and collaboration. The challenges posed by AI are complex and multifaceted, and they require the collective wisdom of individuals from all walks of life. By engaging in open, honest conversations and working together, we can create innovative solutions that address the ethical and societal implications of AI.

Lastly, let's practice self-reflection and cultivate a growth mindset. As we navigate this rapidly changing landscape, it is essential that we remain open to learning, adapting, and evolving. By embracing a growth mindset and constantly reflecting on our actions and choices, we can continue to grow as individuals, while actively contributing to the creation of a more compassionate, inclusive world.

The age of AI presents us with an unprecedented opportunity to shape the future of our society. By embracing empathy, compassion, and unity, we can harness the power of AI to create a world in which every individual is valued, respected, and empowered. Let us seize this moment and work together to build a Gracious Society – one that future generations will look back on with pride, knowing that we made a conscious choice to prioritize human dignity and the common good in the era of AI.

AFTERWARD

Thank you for joining me on this journey as we have explored the potential of AI in fostering a Gracious Society. As we reach the conclusion of this thought-provoking discussion, let us take a moment to envision the future of a Gracious Society powered by AI – a future that not only acknowledges the transformative potential of this technology, but also harnesses it to uplift, empower, and unite people from all walks of life. As we look to the future, we can see a world where AI is used as a force for good – a world where technology is developed with a deep sense of responsibility and a commitment to ethical principles that prioritize human dignity, the common good, and the well-being of our planet.

In this world, AI is utilized to tackle some of the most pressing challenges facing our global community. From combating climate change and protecting our environment to revolutionizing healthcare, education, and social welfare systems, AI has the potential to not only improve the lives of millions but also to create a more just and equitable society.

Imagine a future where AI-driven healthcare systems ensure that everyone, regardless of their socioeconomic background, has access to personalized, data-driven treatments and preventive care. By leveraging AI, we can improve disease detection, optimize treatment plans, and empower patients to take control of their health – ultimately leading to a healthier and happier global population.

Picture a world where AI-powered educational tools provide every student with a personalized learning experience, adapting to their unique strengths and weaknesses to maximize their potential. In this future, barriers to education are broken down, and access to high-quality learning resources is available to all, regardless of their location or economic status.

Envision a planet where AI-driven environmental monitoring and management systems enable us to protect and restore our ecosystems with precision and efficiency. AI can provide us with the tools to predict, model, and mitigate the impacts of climate change, ensuring a sustainable and thriving world for future generations. In the realm of work, AI has the potential to create new job opportunities and industries that we cannot yet imagine. By reskilling and upskilling our workforce, we can ensure that people are prepared to excel in an AI-driven economy – an economy that values creativity, critical thinking, and collaboration.

The future of a Gracious Society powered by AI is one where technology is developed and deployed ethically, with a focus on fairness, transparency, and accountability. In this future, we prioritize the development of AI systems that respect and protect human rights, and we actively work to minimize biases and inequalities.

A Gracious Society of the future emphasizes the importance of collaboration – not only among governments, NGOs, and the private sector but also among individuals from diverse backgrounds and cultures. By fostering a culture of encounter and dialogue, we can learn from one another and work together to ensure that AI is developed and deployed in a manner that benefits all of humanity.

Finally, the future of a Gracious Society powered by AI is one in which each individual plays a crucial role in shaping the world around them. By embracing empathy, compassion, and a growth mindset, we can empower ourselves to make a positive impact in our communities and our global society. As we stand on the precipice of a new era, let us remember that the future is not predetermined. We have the power to shape the world we want to live in – a world where AI is used as a force for good, and where the principles of a Gracious Society are woven into the very fabric of our existence.

To achieve this vision, we must be bold in our aspirations, steadfast in our commitment to ethical principles, and united in our efforts to create a brighter future for all. It is our collective responsibility to ensure that the power of AI is harnessed for the greater good – to build a more compassionate, inclusive, and just society.

As we embark on this journey together, let us remember that the path to a Gracious Society is paved with collaboration, innovation, and a shared commitment to the well-being of all people. Let us learn from each other's experiences, engage in meaningful dialogue, and share our knowledge and resources to overcome the challenges we face. In our pursuit of a Gracious Society, we must be relentless in our efforts to raise awareness about the ethical implications of AI, and to foster a global culture that values empathy, understanding, and human dignity. We must advocate for policies and regulations that ensure AI is developed and deployed in a manner that upholds these values and safeguards the rights of all individuals.

By empowering communities through AI-driven initiatives, we can work towards closing the gap between the rich and the poor, providing everyone with equal opportunities to thrive in a rapidly changing world. This is a vision that transcends borders, cultures, and religions – a vision that unites us all in our shared pursuit of a more just and equitable world.

In the end, the future of a Gracious Society depends on each and every one of us. We must be active participants in shaping the world we want to live in, and we must be willing to confront the challenges that arise along the way. It is only through our collective efforts, our shared commitment to human dignity, and our unyielding determination that we can create a brighter future for all.

So, let us go forth with hope and optimism, confident in our ability to harness the transformative potential of AI in the service of a Gracious Society. Let us be the architects of our own future, building a world that is not only more technologically advanced but also more compassionate, inclusive, and just. Together, we can make this vision a reality – one step, one innovation, and one act of kindness at a time.

Thank you for joining me on this journey, and for your commitment to building a Gracious Society in the era of AI. Let us forge ahead with courage, determination, and a shared sense of purpose – and may our collective efforts inspire generations to come.

RECOMMENEDED READING

Bostrom, N. (2014). **Superintelligence: Paths, Dangers, Strategies.** Oxford: Oxford University Press.

Harari, Y. N. (2015). **Sapiens: A Brief History of Humankind.** Harper.

Kurzweil, R. (2006). **The Singularity Is Near: When Humans Transcend Biology.** Penguin.

McAfee, A., & Brynjolfsson, E. (2017). **Machine, Platform, Crowd: Harnessing Our Digital Future.** W.W. Norton & Company.

Moravec, H. (1999). **Robot: Mere Machine to Transcendent Mind.** Oxford University Press.

Nussbaum, M. (2011). **Creating Capabilities: The Human Development Approach.** Harvard University Press.

O'Neil, C. (2016). **Weapons of Math Destruction: How Big Data Increases Inequality and Threatens Democracy.** Crown.

Raworth, K. (2017). **Doughnut Economics: Seven Ways to Think Like a 21st-Century Economist.** Chelsea Green Publishing.

Sen, A. (1999). **Development as Freedom.** Oxford University Press.

Singer, P. (2010). **The Life You Can Save: How to Do Your Part to End World Poverty.** Random House.

Tegmark, M. (2017). **Life 3.0: Being Human in the Age of Artificial Intelligence.** Vintage.

Zuboff, S. (2019). **The Age of Surveillance Capitalism: The Fight for a Human Future at the New Frontier of Power.** PublicAffairs.

Berggruen, N., & Gardels, N. (2019). **Renovating Democracy: Governing in the Age of Globalization and Digital Capitalism.** University of California Press.

Ehrenreich, B. (2001). **Nickel and Dimed: On (Not) Getting By in America.** Metropolitan Books.

Fromm, E. (1956). **The Art of Loving.** Harper & Row.

Hanh, T. N. (2003). **Creating True Peace: Ending Violence in Yourself, Your Family, Your Community, and the World.** Free Press.

Hinton, S. (2016). **Understanding Context: Environment, Language, and Information Architecture.** O'Reilly Media.

Noddings, N. (1984). **Caring: A Feminine Approach to Ethics and Moral Education.** University of California Press.

Nussbaum, M. (2013). **The Fragility of Goodness: Luck and Ethics in Greek Tragedy and Philosophy.** Cambridge University Press.

Putnam, R. D. (2000). **Bowling Alone: The Collapse and Revival of American Community.** Simon & Schuster.

Sachs, J. (2012). **The Price of Civilization: Reawakening American Virtue and Prosperity.** Random House.

Sen, A. (2009). **The Idea of Justice.** Harvard University Press.

Singer, P. (2009). **The Ethics of What We Eat: Why Our Food Choices Matter.** Rodale Books.

Taylor, C. (2007). **A Secular Age.** Harvard University Press.

References

AI Now Institute. (n.d.). About. Retrieved from https://ainowinstitute.org/about.html

Doctors Without Borders. (n.d.). Who we are. Retrieved from https://www.doctorswithoutborders.org/who-we-are

Feeding America. (n.d.). Our work. Retrieved from https://www.feedingamerica.org/our-work

Future of Life Institute. (n.d.). About FLI. Retrieved from https://futureoflife.org/about/

Habitat for Humanity. (n.d.). About Habitat for Humanity. Retrieved from https://www.habitat.org/about

Khan Academy. (n.d.). Our mission. Retrieved from https://www.khanacademy.org/about

OpenAI. (n.d.). OpenAI Charter. Retrieved from https://openai.com/charter/

Partnership on AI. (n.d.). About us. Retrieved from https://www.partnershiponai.org/about/

Pope Francis. (2020). Fratelli tutti. Retrieved from http://www.vatican.va/content/francesco/en/encyclicals/documents/papa-francesco_20201003_enciclica-fratelli-tutti.html

United Nations. (n.d.). Sustainable Development Goals. Retrieved from https://www.un.org/sustainabledevelopment/sustainable-development-goals/

World Health Organization. (2018). Artificial intelligence (AI) for good global summit. Retrieved from https://www.who.int/news-room/events/detail/2018/05/15/default-calendar/artificial-intelligence-(ai)-for-good-global-summit

Grameen Bank. (n.d.). Bank for the Poor. Retrieved from https://www.grameen.com/

Homeboy Industries. (n.d.). About Us. Retrieved from https://homeboyindustries.org/about/

www.ingramcontent.com/pod-product-compliance
Lightning Source LLC
Chambersburg PA
CBHW020441220526
45464CB00002B/805